GW00702115

To Judy & Stephen
with my very Best
Wishes Gail

COVER: *Cactus Bay*
INSIDE COVER: *The ferry terminal at Matiatia*
TITLE PAGE: *Wharf Road cul de sac*
CONTENTS PAGE: *Sculpture on the Gulf – 'The Kamo Dog' / Barry Lett*
PAGE FOUR: *Satellite Map of Waiheke Island*

In Memory of Michael Thomson

National Library of New Zealand Cataloguing-in-Publication Data

Picard, Stephen
Waiheke Island / text and photography by Stephen Picard.
Includes bibliographical references and index.
ISBN 0-9582182-4-2
1. Waiheke Island (N.Z.) 2. Waiheke Island (N.Z.)—Pictorial
works. 3. Waiheke Island (N.Z.)—Description and travel.
4. Waiheke Island (N.Z.)—History. I. Title.
919.32400222—dc 22

First published in New Zealand 2005
RSVP Publishing Company Limited
PO Box 47 166 Ponsonby, Auckland
www.rsvp-publishing.co.nz

Copyright © 2005 by Stephen Picard

All rights reserved. No part of this book may be reproduced by any means
or in any form whatsoever without written permission from the publisher,
except for brief quotations embodied in literary articles or reviews.

Typeset in Palatino 10 pt
Printed in New Zealand by Brebner Print

Waiheke Island

Texts and Photography
Stephen Picard

RSVP
PUBLISHING

Contents

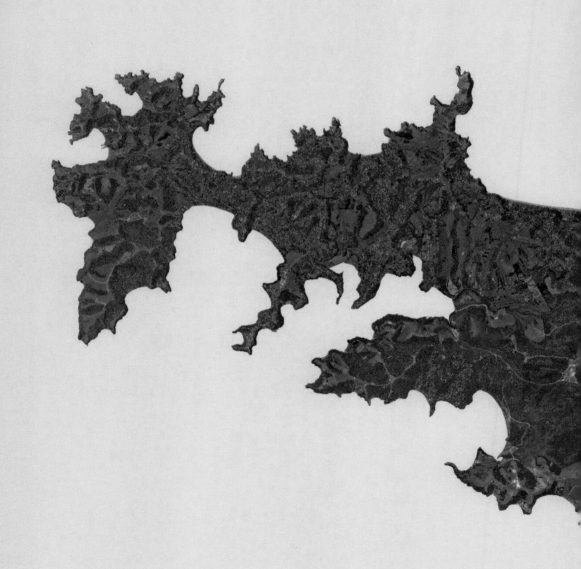

Foreword

I first arrived on Waiheke Island almost 30 years ago one grey Sunday in July on board the *Baroona*. The voyage from Auckland took 80 minutes and it seemed like an eternity, perched in the stern… a real crossing over. My wife and I took a bus out to Onetangi, where we walked the beach. I realised immediately I was home.

Everybody who lives on Waiheke has a similar story of 'enlightenment'. For me — a refugee from London — it was probably the closest I could get back to idyllic childhood holidays on the Isle of Wight and, later when the 1960s ended, an extended summer trip to the Ionian and Aegean islands of Greece.

There's an old question about people who choose to live on islands: 'What are they escaping from?' I suspect, for most people, it's the 'rat race'. In an increasingly depersonalised, global village — where people drive everywhere and never get to know their next-door neighbours — those of us lucky enough to live on islands like Waiheke still live in communities where people share, care and dare to think they can make a difference and a better life for themselves and their families.

Of course, things never remain the same. My first year on the island I was a reporter on the *Auckland Star* and I commuted to work. This entailed catching the *Glen Rosa* (capacity 58 passengers) at 6.15am and 5.15pm every day, or throwing a sickie (some days, literally, even if you caught the ferry!). There were no refreshments — unless you brought your own thermos — only the chance of a fight if you sat in a seat reserved for one of the old card players. Some days it was so rough you arrived at the wharf already soaked to the skin, while other days it was quite dreadful and you were just grateful to arrive in Auckland alive! So nowadays when people complain about a queue at the bar, I remember the *Glen Rosa* and Shorty, who was celebrating 30 years of commuting on the workers' boat. I can't recall what the card players gave him as a gift, but we worked out that Shorty spent three years out of that 30 at sea…

Fortunately, I soon became editor of the *Gulf News* and my commuting days were over. The phone rang 24 hours a day and it became immediately obvious what an amazing and diverse community of souls lived on this beautiful island at the bottom of the world. I felt a feisty independence and generosity of spirit that was everywhere. A Waiheke party has always been something to behold… from toddlers to geriatrics all are welcome, all are valued individuals and all invariably have a good time. It still is that way and I guess it always will be.

Two years ago *On Waiheke Island* went out of print, and the sheer pace of change over the decade indicated to me a completely new book. On the island we might feel sometimes like King Canute trying to hold back the tide of 21st Century suburbanisation, but I for one can only be optimistic about Waiheke's future. When you look at the photographs in this book you will see how the island has changed over 100 years and more… to my mind, we must be doing something right! And the truly encouraging thing is that from whatever background Waiheke Islanders come, the place seems to exercise a peculiar hold on their affections, allied with a fierce loyalty and a desire to leave a better place than they found.

Geography

The island of Waiheke lies 17 kilometres east of Auckland and 15 kilometres west of Coromandel in the Hauraki Gulf, belonging to the North Island of New Zealand.

It is the largest of the 40 or so islands within the Gulf and has 96 kilometres of coastline.

It was known as *Te Motuarairoa*, the long sheltering island — the name bestowed over 600 years ago by the crew of the great Maori canoe *Te Arawa*, who beached at Rangihoua. In the mid-14th Century, a Te Arawa chieftain built a Pa on Maori Hill overlooking Onetangi and renamed the island after himself: *Te Motunui-o-Kahu*, the great island of Kahu. By about 1800 it was known as 'Waiheke', cascading waters and/or ebbing water — perhaps a reference to the importance of the local freshwater supplies — most likely in part to the Europeans, who found it easier to pronounce.

Waiheke is about 92 square kilometres in area, measuring 25 kilometres long and 20 kilometres across at its widest point (though barely one kilometre across at its narrowest). The island comprises 9,324 hectares and has 40 kilometres of beaches, 24 kilometres of tidal flats, 14 kilometres of reserves and 100 kilometres of freehold.

Climate

Waiheke has a maritime climate — warmer temperatures, less humidity, less rain and more sunshine than Auckland.

Records over the past 100 years show average annual rainfall between 865mm and 1,016mm (35 to 40 inches), compared to 1,270mm (50 inches) in Auckland.

The sun shines for an average 2,200 hours per year (2,087 hours in Auckland), and annual temperatures range in the summer (November through March) up to 28 degrees Celsius, down to 11 degrees Celsius in winter (June through August).

OPPOSITE: *Rangihoua (Maori Hill)*

Winds are variable but westerlies to south-westerlies prevail, with the island also exposed to the fierce north-easterlies that sweep in across the Gulf.

Topography

Although Waiheke is "within spitting distance of the biggest city in New Zealand" (attributed to the late 'Hydrofoil Bob' Burns), the view of the Pacific from Oneroa is uninterrupted by any other larger island until it halts at Chile.

The island is circled by delightful beaches. There are fine sandy beaches and many deep sheltered bays which provide good anchorages. The northern coasts contain rocky headlands, making this coastline spectacular and dramatic. The intricately indented coastline of the south creates bays, with mudflats, shellbanks and mangroves.

The soil type on Waiheke is Waitemata sandstone/clay.

Before the arrival of Europeans in the early 1800s much of Waiheke Island was covered in dense native forest, which included many fine kauri trees. Most of the forest was gone by 1850. Now, small pockets of mature bush and areas of swamp are to be found throughout the eastern half of Waiheke. There are remnant forest patches inland, regenerating shrublands and raupo swamps. Much of the rest of the country is farmland and either covered in grass or reverting to bush, and more recently, vineyards.

There were four distinct phases of Maori occupation on Waiheke spanning nine centuries, and the inhabitants left traces of their occupation in the form of archaeological sites scattered across the landscape.

With the coming of the Pakeha, the land was stripped. Between 1850 and 1920 much of the island was cleared and sown for grazing and thus acquired its open rural character.

Settlers were dependent on harvesting the wealth of land and sea. The eastern end was exploited for firewood (tea-tree), manganese and kauri. Most of the forest was felled and cleared. Its place was taken over by the exotic grasses of pastoral farmland and by small settlements of urban development.

OPPOSITE: *Pohutukawa trees in flower between Onetangi and Piemelon Bay*

Prime land for vines alongside Onetangi Straight

By 1900 the island had developed as a sheep farming territory and a holiday destination. Farmland subdivision saw the creation of settlements at Ostend, Onetangi, Palm Beach, Surfdale and Oneroa. Fred Alison bought Oneroa (long, sandy beach) in 1901, farmed and grassed hundreds of acres and sold it in 1922, ushering in the urban development of Waiheke.

Modern Waiheke has seen the western part of the island become a marine suburb of Auckland, with about 1,000 people making a daily, 35-minute ferry commute to town. East Waiheke is still relatively remote and pastoral, resembling the Scottish highlands. The overall impression of the island today is of quiet cottages clustered in settlements, fantasy houses clinging to the hillsides and commanding the ridgelines fringing the beaches, with peaceful pastures undulating down to the coast. The coastscape is an increasingly Mediterranean mix of vineyard and olive plantings.

OPPOSITE: *Looking eastward to Hakaimango Point*
OVERLEAF: *Aerial shot of Oneroa, with Rangitoto Island and Auckland City in the distance*

12

Matiatia

I n the year 2000, a private company — Waitemata Infrastructure Limited — paid $3.5 million for seven hectares of the Matiatia Valley, after Auckland City had earlier offered $1.5 million.

Since then, the fight for the heart and soul of Waiheke's future has been waged at Matiatia — which is entirely appropriate, since it was here that the island's legendary conservationist, Don Chapple planted a small, native forest at Te Atawhai Whenua Reserve, just up the Ocean View Road. Mr Chapple, who died in 2005, was responsible for an estimated 40,000 plantings over a 12-year period at the reserve, which was gifted in the early 1990s to the Royal Forest and Bird Protection Society by Nick and Nettie Johnstone.

The company's initial $35 million development plan envisaged turning the island's gateway into a maritime village incorporating up to 100 multi-storey apartments, shops, restaurants, an underground carpark and a hotel conference centre — the whole complex covering 29,000 square metres (almost three times the permitted site coverage as of right).

Islanders united in fear of the 'Aucklandisation' of their paradise, with 2,275 of Waiheke's 2001 census-night population of 7,137 signing a petition opposing the development (in 10 days), which would have been only a little smaller than the existing commercial centre in Oneroa, one kilometre up the road. CAPOW — the Community and People of Waiheke — was formed to fight the development and protect the island's natural and physical resources "in a sustainable way"; their catch-cry: 'Far enough behind to be ahead'. A 'Love Matiatia' concert raised almost $40,000 in one night.

All but 15 of the 157 submissions opposed the project, and it was turned down by planning commissioners in 2003. They acknowledged local concerns that the development was out of character with Waiheke and would have a negative impact on the environment.

It is a matter of record that it was the people of Waiheke, not the city council, who raised the not-inconsiderable money to put up good lawyers and experts to get some balance at the hearings.

OPPOSITE: The road to Matiatia

Waitemata Infrastructure — a consortium owned by directors of the merchant bank FR Partners — then presented a scaled-back plan from 29,000 square metres of gross floor area to 18,500 square metres (the size of 10 *Placemakers'* buildings). To the alarm of locals, the city council under Mayor Banks signed over one of the two carparks at Matiatia to WIL, and began co-operating with the company on a wastewater treatment plant up the valley, that was perceived as being mostly for WIL's benefit.

The fight rumbled on and in April, 2005, the Environment Court gave the go-ahead to a 10,000 square-metre development of controllable activity, with a further 8,500 square metres of discretionary activity by way of public notification. Public opposition did not abate and in July — to islanders' relief — Mayor Dick Hubbard negotiated a deal under which Auckland City purchased all shares in WIL for $12.5 million.

The city saw Matiatia as a vital strategic asset for the island — its gateway — and Mayor Hubbard pledged it would be developed "in a unique and remarkable way, as the main arrival and departure point for passenger ferries, and the first glimpse of Waiheke Island for visitors from around New Zealand and the world."

Auckland City envisaged a mixed-use development of around 8,000 square metres, with full user-pays parking as part of the deal.

In 2004, almost two million people crossed the wharf at Matiatia.

ABOVE & OPPOSITE: Matiatia & Oneroa Beach, 1928

Villages

Surrounded by the blue waters of the Hauraki Gulf and halfway between Auckland City and the Coromandel Peninsula, Waiheke is both island community and holiday resort.

By 2005 Waiheke Island had reached 90% of its residential capacity (13,000 people under existing subdivision), and consultation on a second major village had begun.

A decision is expected within two years, and the new village is expected to grow up over five to 10 years. It is unlikely to be at the eastern end.

Ostend will have a function in the retail servicing market by virtue of its central position, but it is thought unlikely that it will be allowed to supercede Oneroa's role as the main township.

Town centres such as Oneroa won't be allowed to spread too much. The city council has no preconceived population number for the island. Rather than trying to make it like everywhere else, they are, according to the planning department, "trying to maximize the good things about Waiheke and the opportunities like the wonderful wineries and beaches."

The city council wants to maintain green 'rural belts' — with lower density housing — between each of the existing villages, rather than allowing the villages to merge into one.

The planning department has acknowledged that land prices — which jumped 71% between 1998 and 2004 — will mean Waiheke increasingly becomes the domain of 'monied people'.

Oneroa

Oneroa is the main township and commercial heart of Waiheke, the largest residential settlement and shopping centre in the Gulf.

Subdivided in the 1920s, weekenders could buy sections for 30 English pounds, on five pounds down and five shillings a week.

OVERLEAF: Oneroa Beach at sunset

19

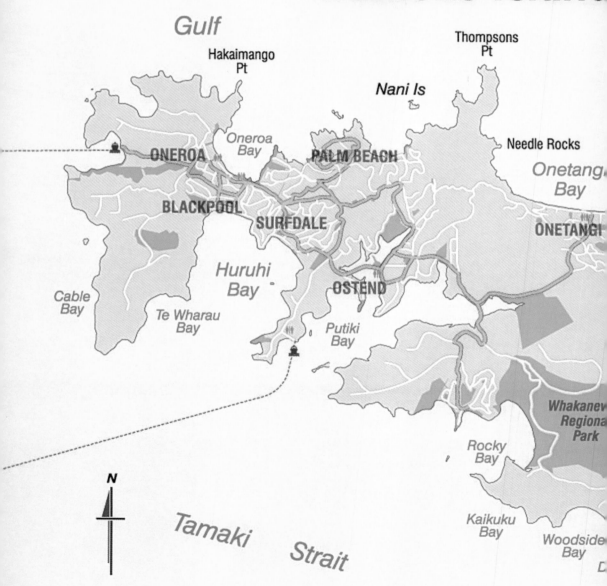

Oneroa village has a most picturesque outlook, sitting overlooking the gentle curve of Oneroa beach and bay. Stepping out of a shop on Ocean View Road one is left in no doubt that this is a Pacific island. The view of Coromandel Peninsula and Great Barrier Island on a clear day is breathtaking.

Oneroa is at its busiest at midday when parking can be a problem; other times it appears dreamy and deserted, even asleep. The buildings are undergoing an ongoing makeover, with recent construction favouring cement plaster and cedar. The village is slowly being transformed — by money, tourism and pastel paint — into a seaside resort with specialty shops, malls, restaurants, winebars and sidewalk cafés.

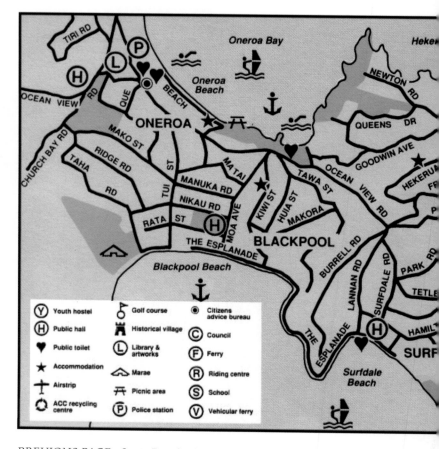

PREVIOUS PAGE: Santa Parade, Oneroa

Oneroa is also home to the banks and real estate agents, plus all of the island's ATM machines, a BP petrol station, the Post Office, the Police, the Citizens' Advice Bureau, an internet café, the Red Cross, the Fire Station, and the library, cinema, information office, radio station, art gallery and theatre at the Artworks complex. And one of the island's two pedestrian crossings (the other is in Ostend).

The commercial portion of Oneroa village is connected to the Owhanake wastewater treatment system. Otherwise, wastewater disposal on the island is reliant in the main on septic tank pre-treatment units and effluent soakage fields. These are required to be pumped out every three years.

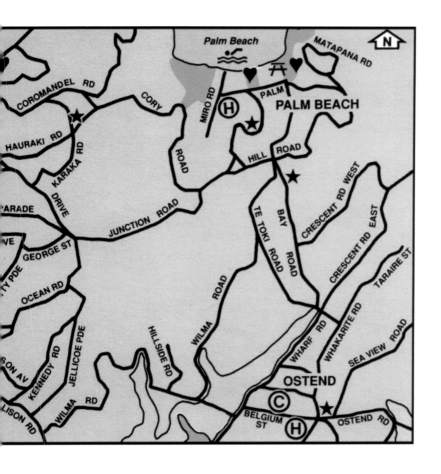

Blackpool

Blackpool is a quiet residential hamlet on the southern down-slope of Oneroa, gathered about the tidal estuary of Huruhi Bay.

It was a thriving Maori settlement in the late 1800s, the site of extensive kumara gardens cultivated by Ngati Paoa, where an old native school operated until 1924.

The Piritahi Marae stands at the western end of the Esplanade, and the Pony Club leases the reserve adjacent to the marae. There is a Maori Cemetery east of Tui Street. The old school is an evocative look at time passing; today, it is used by the Lions Club, and for activities like yoga. In the 1930s, children walked across the marshes to school. The marshland has given way to a wild assortment of homes but something immutable remains. When it rains hard, parts of Blackpool are still water-logged.

Surfdale

In the 1920s Surfdale had a 300ft wharf and steamers called daily over summer. Today, straddling the main road, it has the largest bowling club on the island.

Behind Surfdale's small *locale* of shops, an Irish tavern, Asian noodle and Kiwi takeaways, and an Italian pizzeria, lies the Seaside Sanctuary Rest Home and, further up the beach, the Community Centre along with a children's play park. There is a mini-industrial area up Beatty Parade, and a kindergarden, Te Huruhi School and the Waiheke High School situated on Donald Bruce Road *en route* to Kennedy Point. The Kennedy Point wharf is used by the vehicular ferry service to Half Moon Bay, Panmure, and is Waiheke's main freight supply line to Auckland. Kennedy Point itself was subdivided in the 1970s.

Palm Beach

Palm Beach was christened in the 1920s after the bay's single palm tree. Whether by virtue of its name or its magnificent beach, Palm Beach remains the most popular place to visit for the casual tourist; in the height of summer, being there can sound like a meeting of the United Nations.

At the western end, Little Palm Beach has become probably the most famous nude beach in the Auckland area (there is nude bathing at the western end of Onetangi Beach too) — although an ill-fated attempt to legislate the fact by the 'hippie' county council in 1978 created a national uproar. Behind the beach lies Palm Beach Hall, and at the eastern end is a restaurant/café and a general store.

OPPOSITE & ABOVE: Palm Beach (1928) and today...

Ostend

The Waiheke Sports Club and the Waiheke Boating Club flank Causeway Road. The waters around Putiki Bay form a very popular anchorage and there is a haul-out area at the head of the bay.

On Saturday mornings the Ostend Market is an island institution where you can buy anything and meet everyone — a one-stop shop for fresh food, funky junk and handmade gifts. You might take a pony ride or have your tarot read, eat jam scones or spring rolls, buy organically grown fruit and vegetables, secondhand clothes and hand-me-down nic-nacs, or you might just watch, wonder and enjoy. It's a cavalcade of colour by the RSA on Anzac Reserve.

Ostend is the geographical and administrative centre, home to Auckland City's customer services, quirky shops and bars, pensioner houses, the Community Health Services Centre, the St John's Ambulance Centre, the RSA and the War Memorial Hall. The supermarket and timber yard are big draws at the weekend, lying in the delta before the Tahi Road industrial area adjacent to a skate park and the recycling enclosure and tip. There is a BP petrol station in Albert Crescent.

Rocky Bay

Rocky Bay, also known as Omiha, is renowned for its community spirit and feisty independence — perhaps initially due in part to its relative isolation, for before 1956 when the bridge was built, it could be reached only by boat or on horseback.

Colourful local drama productions are staged at the refurbished hall, but the heart of Rocky Bay was lost to fire in October 2003 when residents watched in horror as flames engulfed their cherished local store/café. The store had only been saved from demolition to make way for townhouses after a concerted local campaign which saw residents keeping a 24-hour watch, sleeping in cars outside the store. This led to Auckland City granting the

ABOVE: *Ostend Market*
OVERLEAF: *Putiki Bay*

31

building heritage status, and the subsequent fire was later confirmed as arson by Police, who found that diesel and petrol were used to incinerate the store. Now only the building's skeleton remains, with the future of the site unclear. No one has been charged in connection with the fire.

Rocky Bay is a good anchorage for yachties, and an annual regatta is a feature of local life. Dirt-track race meetings are held on Sundays at the foot of the Rocky Bay hill. There is a tennis court in Valley Road, and there are some good bush and coastal walks in the area, which is abundant in bird life.

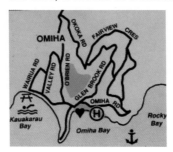

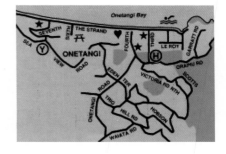

Houseboats at the Rocky Bay turn-off

Onetangi

Onetangi means 'weeping sands'. It boasts the main surf beach on the island where the famous horse races are held every year in late summer, and has a signposted water-ski/surf-ski lane. The waterfront has changed drastically over the past decade: the old beach store has been replaced by a bar/restaurant; the pub has been completely revamped; McGinty's Lodge has been torn down and replaced by 33 luxury apartments, and the Onetangi Hotel, built 1915, also has been converted into luxury accommodation.

The 62-hectare native bush reserve, owned by the Royal Forest and Bird Society in Orapiu Road, has 10 and 90-minute walks though regenerating and mature native forest, and is worth a visit.

There is a Shell petrol station in Onetangi which doubles as a general store, alongside a pizzeria and a liquor outlet. The Youth Hostel, which recently underwent a makeover, is situated at the junction of Seventh Avenue and Seaview Road.

Looking towards Onetangi over the Sports Park from Maori Hill

Orapiu

Orapiu is the most developed settlement in eastern Waiheke, but it is still very small. Orapiu is about a half-hour drive from Oneroa. There are neither shops, cafés nor petrol stations there, so be sure to take your own refreshments... and enough petrol!

There is good fishing from the wharf and at low tide energetic people can take a 45-minute walk around the rocks past Pohutukawa Bay, Otakawhe Bay and Pearl Bay to Te Matuku Bay.

Until recently this was the only ward on the island which consistently voted National. At the general election in September 2005, the Orapiu booth split the vote evenly between National and Labour with 18 votes each; the Greens came in third with 14 votes.

PREVIOUS PAGE: Onetangi panorama

Population

I t's a cosmopolitan lifestyle on Waiheke — a community of broad-minded and liberal people from many cultures and countries. It is both island community and holiday resort. And, as early broadcaster Shirley Maddock pointed out: 'The Island's talent for creating associations is as effortless as breathing'.

The island has been a South Seas refuge, a working-class holiday retreat, a hippie haven, a floating loony-bin. Since the advent of the fast ferry service in the 1980s, there has been an influx of middle-aged and middle-class people, of *nouveau riche* entrepreneurs and developers hoping to make a buck out of the place, and now many residents are afraid to leave their 4WD vehicles unlocked, or their homes without switching on a burglar alarm.

Waiheke folk are proud of saying they make up the third largest island population in New Zealand, and drive around with bumper stickers proclaiming, 'Slow down, you're here'.

Until the watershed of the fast catamaran ferries Waiheke was largely settled by retired people, refugees from city-living, some artists and writers. In response to rapid development, and the threat of cultural uniformity — of becoming merely Aucklanders living on an island in the Gulf, or just another plush beach resort in the Pacific Ocean — there has been a consolidation of the legendary individualism, of the Waiheke identity. Happily the casual, restful atmosphere has survived the commuter invasion and the omens are good. People now come from all walks of life but invariably end up as Waiheke Islanders, no more no less, and all that label entails.

The earliest settlers were the Maruiwi, a people from the East Pacific who arrived about 1,000 years ago. Then came Te Uri Karaka, a semi-nomadic group of hunter/fishers, followed by the descendants of Toi the Navigator; and from about 1300, the Te Arawa people. When Captain Cook's *Endeavour* entered the Gulf in 1769 after his mission to observe the Transit of Venus on Tahiti was completed, the island was the domain of Ngati Paoa.

ABOVE: Peace campaigner Dave Wray

There were thriving Maori communities in the 17th and 18th Centuries, with their palisaded forts and swift canoes, their plantations and villages.

In 1827 French explorer Dumont Durville particularly noticed 'on Wai-Heke sites that would be admirably fitted for settlement'. The first Europeans were sealers and whalers stopping for repairs and potatoes; and the early missionaries. Kauri logging began about 1825.

The first recorded transaction of a European buying land on Waiheke was in 1837 when Thomas Maxwell, a Scot from Aberdeen, claimed 3,000 acres at Man O'War Bay and paid "in goods, 168 pounds and 12 shillings". A whaleboat was also mentioned.

The first recorded European birth on the island was also at Man O'War Bay, on Christmas Day 1841, to Irish immigrants John and Ellen Regan from County Cork — a daughter Mary, who lived to be 101 and had at least 12 children.

Until 1878 Waiheke was known as a place from which firewood came, inhabited by Maori and woodcutters, and by pioneering families scattered in coves. At the time the Reverend F.T. Baker prophetically observed: "A new era has dawned upon Waiheke... It will 'ere long be known as the residence of many a wealthy settler, and from its proximity to Auckland, the beauty of its scenery and climate, cannot fail to be the summer resort of businessmen and their families seeking rest and recreation."

By 1882, when Reverend F. Gould visited the district school, there were 27 children present. About 70 Maori lived in three *kainga* at Te Huruhi, Itangaroa and Matiatia, and there were 34 European settler families.

By 1887 large acreages of timber had been cleared and the estimated population was 80 Maori and 150 Europeans. By 1901 the population was 162 at census.

Ostend and Onetangi were the first areas to be subdivided for settlement in 1916. Oneroa followed in 1922.

ABOVE: *At present, around 70 babies are born on the island each year*
OPPOSITE: *A wedding on Palm Beach*

ABOVE: *Bill Lord, the legendary one-armed saw-doctor*
OPPOSITE: The inaugural Ms Waiheke 1991

The Second World War opened up Waiheke. Petrol was rationed throughout the country and motor travel was almost impossible. Building restrictions were everywhere except on the island, which had virtually no local government or bylaws. By 1945 the standing population was 835, and soon after Waiheke went through a small boom created by Auckland's acute housing shortage and a demand for land for holiday purposes.

By 1956 the population had climbed to 2,000; to 2,300 by 1966; to 3,500 by 1978; to 4,543 by 1986; to 5,924 by 1990; and to 7,500 by 2001. By 2005 it stood around 8,000, with 85% of sites occupied. The latest estimate projects a possible population of 12,350 by 2020. The increasing popularity of the island has seen pre-school, kindergarden, primary, intermediate and high school rolls mushroom, and led to a new primary school opening in Seaview Road in 2005, with an intended roll of 500.

There are three retirement villages on the island.

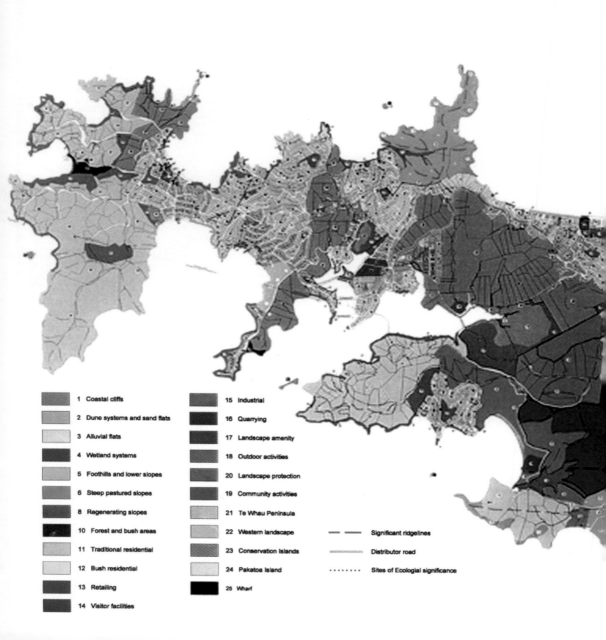

1	Coastal cliffs	15	Industrial
2	Dune systems and sand flats	16	Quarrying
3	Alluvial flats	17	Landscape amenity
4	Wetland systems	18	Outdoor activities
5	Foothills and lower slopes	20	Landscape protection
6	Steep pastured slopes	19	Community activities
8	Regenerating slopes	21	Te Whau Peninsula
10	Forest and bush areas	22	Western landscape
11	Traditional residential	23	Conservation islands
12	Bush residential	24	Pakatoa Island
13	Retailing	25	Wharf
14	Visitor facilities		

Significant ridgelines

Distributor road

Sites of Ecologial significance

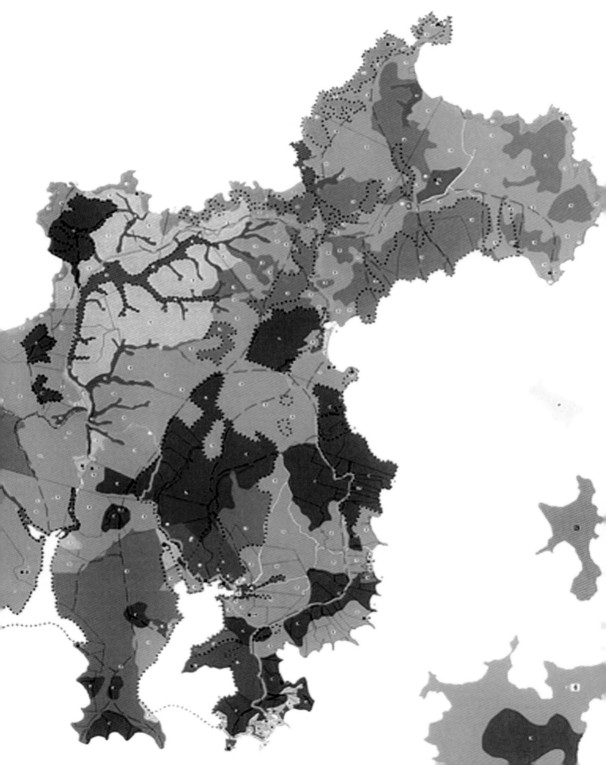

ABOVE: *Sandra Lee addressing an Anzac Day commemoration*
PREVIOUS PAGE: *The 2005 land use map of Waiheke Island*

Politics

Waiheke was one of the last places in New Zealand to gain local government; prior to 1921 there were no bylaws whatsoever. The island was then administered by roads boards for almost 50 years — first the Ostend and the Orapiu, then the Western Waiheke, and finally the Waiheke — and the name reflected the local body's main spheres of operation — roads, rates and rubbish — until the Waiheke County Council was born in 1970. The county council lasted 19 years until the island became a ward of Auckland City.

A look at the historical ledger reveals some interesting snippets. In 1932, Ostend Roads Board chairman Francis Brown reported with satisfaction that several roads had been metalled, bringing the total mileage of metalled roads to nearly 12 miles.

In 1945 the island's 835 residents rejected a merger with Auckland City. In 1946, the board purchased the Rangihoua quarry site for 135 pounds.

The 1948/9 accounts show estimated income at 4,720 pounds from metal, rent, building permits, a rates subsidy, a main highway subsidy, licences and rates, with estimated expenditure of 4,600 pounds, covering wages, legal expenses, office stationery, tools, a truck, insurance and building repairs.

By 1961/2, estimated expenditure had grown to 54,276 pounds, covering the board's administration, inspection services (health, building, traffic, noxious weeds, dog registration and the dog pound), town planning, real estate purchases (the Oneroa reserve), loan charges, works department plant, and repairs to the Orapiu wharf.

Today many Waiheke street names recall past chairmen of the roads boards and county council, including McIntosh Road, Woollams Road, Garratt Road, Brown Road, Giles Road, Le Roy Road, McMillan Road, Newton Road and Donald Bruce Road.

The county council had a most colourful history, beginning April 1, 1970, with Jack McIntosh — a grandson of W. N. McIntosh who chaired the first Orapiu Roads Board from 1921 to 1933 — presiding as chairman for the last two years of the roads board and the first seven of the council. His time in office was dominated by island dissatisfaction with the Waiheke Shipping Company's licensed monopoly. At licensing authority hearings, company owner Leo Dromgoole was accused of creaming off profits from the Waiheke run to subsidise his unprofitable Devonport service, and to buy land on Rakino Island (he denied both claims). Islanders implored him to replace his ageing Waiheke fleet with modern, faster vessels, but to no avail.

'Big Jack' was succeeded in 1977 by 28-year old Kerry Greer, who became the youngest county chairman in New Zealand history. Mr Greer's tenure attracted national interest from newspapers such as *Truth* and *Sunday News* over issues like nude bathing, and came to an unfortunate end after one term. He was subsequently convicted of importing drugs and was sent to prison in 1980.

In an astonishing sequel, his successor Ron Gay was also arrested — after just two months as county chairman — and was convicted of a smuggling offence involving the importation of firearms and stereos from Fiji. Mr Gay was fined and his yacht was confiscated.

Under Ian Faulconbridge, Alan Murray and Sandra Lee, Waiheke's fortunes prospered through the 1980s with commercial growth and increasing population — largely due to an influx of the young and middle-aged, the sale of Mr Dromgoole's ferry companies to Fullers, and their introduction of new, fast ferries. The legal battle with John Spencer over possession of roads through his farmland around Stony Batter also began at this time.

The Spencer sage took more than 10 years and cost ratepayers over $1 million. It ranks as the perfect illustration of the sheer bloody-mindedness of island politics. In short, rumblings began in 1970 when the county council started work on the 7.9-kilometre loop road from Cowes Bay north to Man O'War Bay. Completed two years later, it allowed motorists to drive right around Waiheke. However, when Mr Spencer (the richest man in New Zealand at the time) bought the land through which the loop road runs in 1980, he discovered no official record of the road ever having been officially registered as public property. In September 1992 he had the loop road blocked at both ends with earth mounds and locked gates, and from that time on unofficial war was declared by angry residents as the city undertook legal action. Though the High Court ruled against Mr Spencer in 1996, he took the case to appeal — which he lost — and then to the Privy Council in London (where he lost again), thereby tying up the issue (and the road) in red tape until 2002. A direct repercussion of this for islanders was

A Green Party 'State of the Nation' address at Surfdale Reserve

the loss of direct access by land to Cactus Bay — one of the most beautiful beaches on Waiheke (see *COVER*). The old track is now a vineyard; the only way to enjoy Cactus Bay is by boat.

The island's volatile politics were also reflected by a judicial inquiry into a county council election, and one resident had the dubious distinction of being the only person in New Zealand to be prosecuted under the Election and Polls Act.

Waiheke's first and last county chairwoman, Sandra Lee, became the island's first ward Auckland City councillor in 1989, following amalgamation. Neither Ms Lee, the island nor the city sought the shake-up in local government which led to the county council's demise, but a subsequent call for de-amalgamation failed to restore its independence. The county council's voice has since been heard through the Waiheke Community Board, and the councillor for the Hauraki Gulf Islands, Faye Storer.

OPPOSITE: Gun emplacement at Stony Batter

Ms Lee, meanwhile, was elected deputy-leader of both the Alliance and Mana Motuhake, and in 1993 she stood for Parliament and defeated Labour's Richard Prebble in Auckland Central. She became a cabinet minister under Helen Clark and later became New Zealand's consular representative on Niue Island.

Political interest continues to run hot on Waiheke, with the Gulf Islands Ward invariably having the largest percentage turnout and the highest number of contestants of any ward in Auckland City.

Surprisingly, only 61% of eligible voters voted on Waiheke in the September 2005 general election — down from 68.2% in 2002. Labour received 44%, National 25% and the Greens 19% of the island vote.

The carved pawaka at Piritahi Marae

Maoritanga

There were four distinct phases of Maori occupation on Waiheke spanning nine centuries, and their history follows the classical pattern of one tribe conquering and ousting the other.

Maruiwi, a people from the East Pacific, settled on Waiheke about 1,000 years ago. Maori legend has it that Kupe visited the island about this time. The local tribe were Te Uri Karaka (the descendants of Karaka, a Maruiwi ancestor). They were skilled fishermen and expert makers of nets and mats, who sailed double canoes and rafts of interlaced flax stalks and raupo leaves, practiced no agriculture except for cultivation of the hue (gourd), and were adept with the sling-spear.

Coming from island groups in Eastern Polynesia, hunter-fisher-gatherer bands scattered around the coast of the island for two centuries.

The second phase saw Toi the Navigator arrive from Hawaii, and a few of his people settled on the island circa 1200AD. Around this time Waiheke was the scene of a terrible massacre. A party of Maraetai Maori led by Chief Maeaea accepted an invitation to a feast from the Waiheke people at Omaru. They sailed across the Tamaki Strait in canoes, but as they landed on the beach at Woodside Bay they were enclosed in hand-nets and speared. This episode was later avenged by a war party which travelled more then 200 miles from Whakatane.

In the middle of the 14th Century *Te Arawa*, the great voyaging double canoe, arrived via Rarotonga from Tahiti, and there emerged greater cultural sophistication in Maori life. It was an era of Pa building, and alliances between neighbours to maintain security. At the end of its migrating voyage, *Te Arawa* paused in Putiki Bay before sailing on to Maketu in the Bay of Plenty, stopping on the way at Moehau (Coromandel) where a colony was founded, named Huarere, who became dominant and the recognised owners of all the Hauraki Gulf. The Ngati Huarere occupied Waiheke for over a century. They developed fortified Pa sites; one of them being Maori Hill at the head of Putiki Bay.

Waiheke was invaded by Ngati Awa from Taranaki around 1650. The Ngati Paoa from Hauraki took over a short time later; their

Piritahi Marae

tribal heartland lay between the Pa on Whakatiwai and the Piako River. Their population probably exceeded 2,000 before the end of the 17th Century.

Hongi Heke captured and destroyed Putiki Pa in 1821, and his war parties devastated the other Waiheke settlements.

The first Christian convert was William Jowett (Wiremu Hoete), a Maori teacher at Putiki. Many Maori followed his example and Waiheke's first church was probably established by Ngati Paoa at Church Bay in 1833, site of the biggest settlement.

In the 1840s Maori from Te Huruhi and most of the other Waiheke bays traded kumara, potatoes, corn and firewood with settlements in Auckland and Maraetai.

By 1860 the Pakeha population had gained over Maori, and tension between the races increased. The King movement was forced from the Waikato by Imperial troops, resulting in a land confiscation which plunged the Waikato people into despair. The Ngati Paoa were also affected and they vacated Waiheke.

By 1916 most of the Maori families had sold their land and left Waiheke, settling in the Miranda district. Not long after, the native school at Blackpool was abandoned.

Today, a Marae — Piritahi Marae — has been re-established at Blackpool, and Waiheke Station — the 2,890-acre Maori Affairs farm — has been handed back to the Ngati Paoa as a result of a Waitangi Tribunal decision, after the Waiheke community successfully argued against a proposal that would have seen the land sold to an individual Maori.

In 1995 the Maori Queen, Dame Te Atairangikaahu opened the new Kohanga Reo at the marae during her visit to the island.

In 2000, Piritahi Marae's new health clinic was opened by the Associate Minister of Maori Affairs (and former Waiheke County Chairwoman) Sandra Lee.

Two years later an 80-member hikoi marched from the marae to Te Huruhi School to protest Education Minister Trevor Mallard's decision not to 'recapitate' the Kohanga Reo. His decision meant bilingual pupils remain split between the primary and high schools.

A group of Tibetan Buddhists stayed on the marae for a fortnight and created a sand 'Love Mandala' for New Zealand, which they deposited in Huruhi Bay. The mandala is pictured on page 137

Most easily recognisable monuments of the pre-European past are the Pa or defended sites which are found on many of the narrow headlands of Waiheke. A 1975 archaeological survey identified 20 Pa sites; many were found in association with the estuarine bays on the south side of the island. Since then the number identified has more than doubled. The most accessible is down a path which provides public access between Silver Bay and Pasadena Bay.

These Pa were defended by the construction of a ditch and bank which cut the headland off from the mainland. Other sites, located on ridges inland from the coast, were more difficult to defend and more elaborately built with double ditch and bank sequences.

Many of the defended headland sites show evidence of being carefully planned to overlook each other and the bays around them. This is demonstrated at Te Whau Point and Korakorahi Point. Mount Maunganui — at 231 metres (759ft), the highest point on the island — was once a fortified Pa site, where one can look across to the Manukau Heads beyond the isthmus. Another Pa site hard to overlook is Rangihoua above the mangrove-fringed inlets of Putiki Bay, claimed by Te Arawa in the 14th Century.

As well as the fortified sites, there are traces of villages which are generally seen as pit and terrace sites, or places where houses and storage facilities were constructed. The majority of the pit sites (which were used for food storage) are found in concentrations; the first about Owhiti Bay, the next at Hooks and Man O'War bays, along the ridgetop between Cowes Bay and Orapiu, and lastly in the middle region of the Awaawaroa Valley beyond and adjacent to Maunganui. Sometimes gardens are found near the village sites. These can be identified on the slopes of each valley.

A further feature left by the pre-European occupants on Waiheke are the rubbish dumps or middens. They were located on beachfronts, sand dunes, estuary shores and inland; the contents were shells, bone (fish and human), hangi stones, and obsidian.

Maori graves can be found inland from Te Wharau Bay and at the end of Tahatai Road.

Often found on the island are tools used by the occupants, such as obsidian or black volcanic glass which originates from Mayor Island and the Great Barrier areas. The majority of adzes were made from local Motutapu greywacke. Greywacke flakes are readily found on Waiheke beaches. Jasper has been found in archaeological sites on Waiheke — for instance, near Stony Batter — where some of the stones show evidence of having been struck and flaked in order to make a useful tool for cutting, scraping or drilling.

Hooks Bay and Thumb Point, with Horuhoru Rock (Gannet Rock)

Colonial History

T he chart of Captain Cook's *Endeavour* records that on his way up the east coast of the North Island in 1769, Cook obtained water from a place he described as 'the black rocks' — a landfall that local history assigns to the Opopo Bay spring.

In November 1820, Samuel Marsden found Waiheke appeared as large as the Isle of Wight. A visiting Englishwoman at this time described the shores as bold and craggy and thickly timbered to the water's edge. That same year Waiheke was offered to Major Cruise and his party in exchange for one musket!

In 1826 Captain Herd from Leith, Scotland, on board the *Rosanna*, was dispatched by the New Zealand Association to purchase land for settlement, consisting initially of the Hauraki islands. Waiheke was referred to as 'Whyeckee', and abundant timber trees were the attraction.

The consideration given for these islands consisted of a double-barrelled gun, eight muskets and a barrel of powder.

Captain Herd was greeted by a haka on arrival, which created dismay. The *Rosanna* departed without landing, for the Bay of Islands. A few plucky ones disembarked there and walked overland to Hokianga to settle at Horeka and began timber and shipbuilding trades.

The earliest European settler on Waiheke was Thomas Maxwell, who settled at Te Matuku Bay about 1825. He married the daughter of a Maori chief and built and launched the island's first sailing vessel.

About this time kauri logging began. Settlers wanted kauri for shipbuilding, and later for building houses; when it was gone they became gumdiggers, and then sheepfarmers.

Te Matuku Valley supported a kauri forest and early European bushmen and traders sold kauri logs to Auckland, Australia, the United States and the United Kingdom.

Logan Campbell described a kauri taken aboard the *Delhi* for Sydney. The longest spar of the cargo was 25 metres long, hauled out by a Maori tribe of 80 or more men.

Man O'War Bay became the centre where giant kauri trees were hauled out to supply masts for British Navy ships. Rafts were towed to the Kauri Timber Company in Auckland by the paddle steamer *Lyttleton*.

The best wood was taken by 1850 for wooden towns on both sides of the Tasman. Bullock teams hauled a wagon of kauri, rimu and totara logs to the head of Te Matuku Bay. On the northern ridge above Hekerua and Sandy bays there was a tramway for logs, which were sent crashing over a convenient cliff to the beach below.

Puriri was felled for house foundations, fenceposts and battens. Much of the bush cover was sold for firewood; vast areas of manuka provided fuel for Auckland stoves and parlour fires, and was also used for ladies' irons and garden stakes. In 1898, 1,000 tons of tea-tree firewood was advertised at nine shillings to 10 shillings per ton at the Auckland wharf.

When the supply of kauri began to dwindle, farming activity increased and settlement was accelerated by indiscriminate clearing of the remaining forest. Digging for kauri gum ('poor man's gold') — which was used for industrial processing, particularly in the manufacture of paint and polishes, and for kindling sluggish fire — was a profitable sideline while the land was being brought into production. The hills around Surfdale, and especially in the eastern

Man O'War Bay

half of the island where the kauri had flourished, were full of little pits where the gumdiggers were working.

Small quantities of gold were found near Cowes Bay and manganese was mined at Awaawaroa ('long valley'); mainly pick and shovel work turning out 45 tons weekly. The seam was discovered in 1839 by Henry Taylor, who started the first copper company at Kawau Island. Later there was a small manganese mine above Owhiti Bay, from which manganese was sent by flying fox to waiting boats; it was most frequently used as ballast in sailing ships, as an oxide in bleaching powders and glass-making, and as an essential ingredient in the Bessemer process for steel-making (patented in 1856). The mine in the Awaawaroa Valley at the foot of Mount Maunganui was New Zealand's largest manganese mine until it closed in 1896 — when the ore was fetching just two pounds a ton.

There was also a limited amount of mining for jasper, silver and copper.

By 1860 a small store at Awaawaroa stocked staples including bags of saltbeef, salt, flour, tea, sugar and hops, boots and laces, lamp globes, pills, pipes and plug tobacco.

Shingle from the beaches fuelled Auckland's building boom (Grafton Bridge and the railway wharf in Auckland are examples constructed with the help of shingle removed from Woodside Bay and Omaru Bay). The shingle was often stolen by moonlight with the skippers promising payment when tackled, but often forgetting. The removal of shingle off the beach at Hooks Bay in time saw the sea — freed from its natural boundaries — advance to engulf 20 acres of foreshore, submerging sheepyards, orchard, flower and vegetable gardens. The house itself was towed to higher ground by a bullock team.

Acacia Cottage — the home of Sir John Logan Campbell — was built in 1841 from Waiheke kauri and now nestles in Cornwall Park.

Windswept Hooks Bay, at the eastern tip of Waiheke, welcomed its first Pakeha settlers in the 1860s. Its first European owner, A. Shepherd, sold 610 acres (at five shillings an acre) to John Hooks.

A 22-room, kauri villa on 400 acres at Pipitewai Bay, prior to restoration

By 1865 European settlement on the island had shifted to Onetangi. Typical early settler lifestyle saw tea-tree cut and sold as firewood, pasture developed for sheep, a few cattle and pigs were kept, homemade butter was produced, and a big vegetable garden was tended along with fruit trees so that fruit could be dried for preservation.

Work was clearly defined. Men's work was fishing, clearing land for hill-country sheepfarming, felling, cutting and selling wood. Woman's work involved caring for their large families and the farm animals, pulling scrub, milking the cows, making the butter and tending the orchard and gardens.

Graves at the Te Matuku Bay Pioneer Cemetery date from 1886. The coffins were brought up a winding creek by rowing-boat, and funeral guests had to wait 12 hours for another full tide to leave.

The first and only British royal visit to Waiheke occurred in 1869 when *HMS Galatea* anchored at Hooks Bay and the Duke of Edinburgh disembarked and had a cup of tea at the homestead with Mrs Jane Hooks.

The settlers relied on the steamers which plied the Waiheke Channel for contact with the mainland. By the late 1870s the cutters operated a postal service to Putiki and Woodside Bay settlements. The first Waiheke Post Office was opened in 1876. The postmaster had to row out to collect mail from the passing steamers. Three early post offices were at Putiki, Cowes Bay and Awaawaroa and they were destined to become early telephone exchanges.

In the early days Oneroa was a wheat-growing area. The land at Matiatia was all Maori property divided into 38 blocks and governed by two chiefs. The biggest settlement was at Church Bay.

With the sea around Waiheke teeming with snapper, many settlers built smokehouses and supplied smoked fish to the Auckland market. Flounder was easily caught by spear or net in the shallow bays. Sharks were used for garden manure. Rock oysters, mullet and sprats were bountiful. Mussels were steamed open and packed into casks for export to China from a small factory in Mussel Heap Bay between Orapiu and Omaru Bay.

One couple camped in Putiki Bay and made brooms using beach rushes with tea-tree handles; and rushes and flax were woven into mats and baskets.

The first settler school opened in Te Matuku Bay in 1882 with 27 pupils. It was established with the help of a visiting Anglican parson after the Gordons made a room available in their home.

School picnic at Cowes Bay, 1902

Waiheke's first regatta was held at Man O'War Bay on December 28, 1882, and the *S.S. Coromandel* was chartered to bring 100 passengers over from Auckland. The first horse race meetings also began around 1880 on Onetangi Beach.

The Browns became the first Europeans to live at Piemelon Bay — once famous for its melons, which were made into jam with a little ginger for flavouring and sweetness — in 1883.

By the turn of the century the island had developed as sheepfarming territory and a holiday destination. Cowes Bay was a favourite spot for excursionists, complete with boarding house, an asphalt bicycle track, a long wharf with kauri piles, and a dance and band rotunda built on the flat.

ABOVE: Thompsons Point
OVERLEAF: *Looking eastward at the Puke Range from Awaawaroa Road*

61

Tourist Trophy motorcycle races, Ostend, January 1931

The undisputed king was Len Perry, who won eight races and set the course record of six minutes 20 seconds in 1947. He rode on 350cc and 500cc Velocette bikes.

1930 — The Depression forced prices down; much of the island was now subdivided.

Home-killed meat was sold by several farmers; also eggs and fruit.

Topdressing raised stock numbers on marginal farmland. The first airstrip was on a rise near the road from Onetangi; followed by one on an Orapiu headland.

District Nurse Gladys Tribe travelled her rounds on horseback.

In 1936, eastern Waiheke and Ponui settlers provided finance to start the Waiheke Passenger Service Limited, and the *Baroona* — a steam trawler used for Seine fishing in the Gulf — was purchased. The skipper was Arthur Day.

The old Blackpool School opened. It found a new lease of academic life in 2005 as temporary site for the Waiheke Primary School, while the new school was being finished in Seaview Road.

OVERLEAF: Putiki Bay

A slaughterhouse was built at Matiatia. It remained an iconic feature of the Ocean View Road landscape until 2004, when it was overturned by vandals using a digger nearby.

The Awaawaroa Bay guesthouse closed; also Te Matuku School.

Efficient dairy farms were run in Ostend and Onetangi until pasteurisation became compulsory in the 1960s.

Johnny Wray, the author of *South Seas Vagabonds*, and his wife Loti, were the first to build in Shelly Beach Road in 1936.

1940 — The Police Station shifted to Oneroa in 1942. That year work also began on the Stony Batter defence establishment.

The *Waiheke Resident* started printing in 1947.

The *Iris Moana* began a daily workers' ferry service to the city from Surfdale in 1948.

Telephones were installed in 1949.

1950 — The first underwater electricity pipeline from Maraetai was laid in 1950; the second in 1966. Electric power came to the island in 1957. Prior to that, cooking was done on coal, wood and even oil-fired stoves. Cool rooms were operated by petrol motors, and 240v DC generators were installed for lighting.

1951 saw the opening of St Peter's Catholic Church in Oneroa and the Anglican Church of the Transfiguration on a rise overlooking Alison Park.

1952 saw the inaugural meeting of the Waiheke Volunteer Fire Brigade.

Captain Fred Ladd started an amphibian seaplane service to Surfdale from Mechanics Bay in 1955.

The council offices in Belgium Street were built in 1957.

In 1958 the Royal Forest and Bird Protection Society bought a 65-hectare reserve at Onetangi, featuring the only stand of mature kauri at the western end of the island.

1960 — The causeway across the Okahuiti Creek in Ostend was constructed in 1961.

A road from Onetangi to Cowes Bay was put through in 1965.

An oyster farm, covering eight acres in Putiki Bay, started up in 1965. In its first 10 years of operation it yielded approximately 6,000 sacks, most of which were exported to Hong Kong.

The O'Brien family sold 2,500 acres of land at Omiha to the Rothschilds.

Auckland Anglican Diocese began running adventure camps

District Nurse Gladys Tribe with 'Patches', her first horse; 1939

in 1967 at Simkin House in Palm Beach.

A hydrofoil service to Auckland City began in 1967.

A Red Cross 'Meals on Wheels' service began in 1968.

1970 — The Red Cross opened a recreation centre in the former Ascot Picture Theatre.

Fire destroyed the Orapiu Hotel.

The *Waiheke Settler* established in 1970, three years before *Gulf News*.

Kennedy Point, Wilma Road, Junction Road and Thompsons Point all subdivided in 1973.

The hydrofoil *Manu-Wai* made its last run to Waiheke in December, 1973.

Direct phone dialling to Auckland arrived in December, 1976.

Connells Store opened in 1904 and closed in 1977.

Kim and Jeanette Goldwater, inspired by the Bordeaux winemakers, established cabernet sauvignon stock in Ostend.

Work started on the Matiatia to Oneroa footpath in 1978.

The hovermarine *Wakatere* started a short-lived Waiheke service.

The hovermarine Wakatere

1980 — The Rothschilds sold their land at Omiha to Chris Reeve.

The Hudson family took over the ferry service in August, 1981.

The Area School split into Te Huruhi School and Waiheke High School in 1985.

The $2.4 million *Quickcat*, built in Perth, began the Auckland service in 1987.

GULF NEWS

JANUARY 20, 1978   20 CENTS

HIGH NOON IN THE RANGITOTO CHANNEL
Battle of the Gulf

A telegram sent by the Peace Squadron to the Pope, and a message of warning to protesters from the Prime Minister, Mr Muldoon, could not avert a desperate confrontation this week in the Rangitoto Channel over the visit of the American nuclear submarine USS Pintado.

On Monday at 12.02pm, the submarine was met by a peace flotilla of 120 boats, strung across the entrance of Auckland harbour in a 1½ km line from Takapuna beacon through 'A' buoy to Rangitoto Island.

The submarine was led into port by the naval frigate Waikato. It was flanked by seven harbour patrol boats and the Police launch Deodar. Two Navy helicopters provided air support.

For many of the protesters, the Pintado's arrival ended a long vigil. "Operational reasons" saw the submarine's arrival delayed by two days (while Navy divers checked the harbour floor around its proposed berth at Jellicoe Wharf), and some members of the Peace Squadron were out at daybreak anxious that the nuclear vessel might slip into port before its scheduled time.

CONTINUED ON PAGE 2 ▶

Holy Mackerel! Is it a bird? Is it a plane? Is it Moby Dick?

Island affairs have been mirrored every week for over 30 years by Gulf News — from early days as a 10-cent offset through to today's sophisticated, colour Apple Mac production. Its independence has ruffled a few feathers along the way, but it has survived the nuclear debate, having to print off-shore to escape the county's area of control, and even Rob Muldoon's election barn-storming on the island...

73

The last eastern post office closed at Connells Bay in 1987. Further closures left the island with only the one post office in Oneroa.

Waiheke County Council adopted a seven-year spraying ban on herbicides in 1988. A year later, it was swallowed up by the Auckland City Council.

The Ostend dump became the Refuse Management Station in 1989 when recycling officially began.

1990 — A cultural and recreation centre, Artworks opened on the former Mitre 10 site at Oneroa in October 1991, and Gulf Radio started transmitting next door a year later.

A new Whare-nui was built on Piritahi Marae, by donations and voluntary labour.

City council pensioner units were built in Belgium Street.

Matiatia's new $2.375 million wharf opened in 1993.

Anzac Bay boat owner Gary Moulton towed his vessels *Phoenix* and the 100ft *Zeus* to the Coromandel Peninsula after years of foreshore occupancy and three orders to leave from the Planning Tribunal.

Leo Dromgoole — who purchased the Waiheke Shipping Company in 1968 — died in 1993, aged 81.

Police burnt 490 cannabis plants found on the island, worth an estimated $500,000.

Island home milk deliveries — which peaked in 1982 when the eastern end had 800 deliveries daily and the western had slightly more — ended.

Traffic density on Waiheke was increasing 17% per annum.

In 1993 the burglary rate on the island was three times the national average.

The 70-year old Onetangi Hotel was sold at auction. It had a government valuation of $2.7 million.

Demographics for the Gulf showed Waiheke had a high proportion of non-car owning residents, divorcees, home-owners and income-support recipients. Waiheke also had the lowest average personal income in Auckland — $13,791, compared with $20,622 for Auckland City as a whole.

By 1995 commercial rates had soared by up to 520% in three years, with commercial ratepayers paying virtually the same as their mainland counterparts despite having no sewage or water reticulation and an entirely different population base.

The 15-hectare Kauakerau Forest on Te Whau Point finally became

The 15-hectare Kauakerau Forest on Te Whau Point finally became a reserve after 13 years of discussion.

Local resident Gu Cheng — one of the most well-known of China's 'misty' poets — attacked his wife Xie Ye with an axe and then hung himself at Ostend in a shocking murder-suicide that stunned the community.

Exceptional bursary results saw Waiheke High School become the fourth highest scorer in the country out of 365 state secondary schools in 1996.

A disputed jetty at Waikopou Bay was demolished by chainsaw-wielding residents after obtaining sanction from the Auckland Regional Council.

Plans to subdivide the north-west tip between Matiatia and Owhanake and Park Point were unveiled.

Waiheke historian Dixie Day, QSM — author of the authoritative *Waiheke Pioneers* — died in 1997, aged 82.

1998 recorded the driest summer since 1957.

Fullers were taken over by Stagecoach — the New Zealand arm of the British operator — with the Hudson family remaining in day-to-day control.

Oneroa-Surfdale Transport left its Blackpool depot after 40 years, in favour of Ostend.

Fullers new *Superflyte* ferry arrived from its Perth shipyard.

Island identity Bill Belcher — the single-handed yachtsman who survived 28 days at sea in a life-raft after his boat was wrecked on the notorious Middleton Reef in the Tasman Sea — died in hospital, aged 87.

Woolworths took over the New World Supermarket in Ostend.

An Onetangi property owner was fined $18,000 for removing the limbs from a neighbour's pohutukawa tree.

And by the turn of the new century, Waiheke gained its first pedestrian crossing, at Oneroa.

ABOVE: An unconventional Waiheke bus stop
OVERLEAF: Sixty years on... from Onetangi Beach, 1933

The Millennium

The eve of a new century on Waiheke was subdued owing to inclement weather. *Gulf News* reported it "quiet, wet, eerie and introspective". Perhaps, in retrospect, a moment of calm before the quickening pace of change kicked in…

The harbingers were not far off — the new owners of the Harbour Master's site at Matiatia announced they were not planning anything "high density", with director Stephen Norrie quoted as saying they were looking for "a Bay of Islands feel".

A major lifestyle subdivision in Church Bay was given the go-ahead by the Environment Court after three years of court wrangling, and the new $4 million Onetangi Sports Park opened in August — with the first ever NPC rugby game to be held on the island two days later, seeing Canterbury defeat Auckland 34-28.

A 700-signature petition urging the community board to build the island's long-awaited skatepark was dismissed as "a publicity stunt" by board chairman Bruce Bissett. The skatepark later went ahead at Ostend

In October islanders grieved the loss of Tim Hubbard, a much-loved island identity and former community board chairman, after he drowned in a boating accident off Ostend.

In 2001 an Auckland City meeting was disrupted by protesters against Oneroa's $2.6 million wastewater system being taken over by Metrowater, and the Waiheke Volunteer Coastguard won Auckland Coastguard's top award after rescuing a stricken launch and her five crew.

Four new 'all-weather' tennis courts at the sports park opened amid high praise for the $300,000 synthetic 'astroturf' surface.

Tributes flowed after the deaths of yachtsman and peace campaigner Dave Wray, broadcaster and author of *Islands of the Gulf*, Shirley Maddock, former fighter pilot and 'squire of Awaawaroa', Larry Lorrigan, and former fire chief Stan White.

Local boxer Daniel Codling finished an unbeaten year at the Oceania Games (and later won a bronze medal at the Manchester Commonwealth Games).

OPPOSITE: 'Fashion Addiction' at Artworks

Superman (Peter Franken) in the field at the Onetangi beach races

By 2002 the city's rate take from Waiheke had doubled in eight years to $5 million. Artworks Cinema laid claim to being the first in the world to screen *Lord of the Rings: The Two Towers*, and islanders concerned about Waiheke youths launched Friends of the Street — a programme aimed at getting youth at risk home safely.

Auckland City confirmed its plans to buy Artworks for $1.2 million; an eight-metre great white shark was inadvertently caught in a net off Gannet Rock; Northpower pleaded guilty in the Auckland District Court to two charges of illegally clearing native bush on Waiheke; and the Ministry of Education installed a statutory manager at Waiheke High School in the wake of controversy and staff unrest.

In the five years to 2005, the Westpac Rescue Helicopter flew 769 missions to Waiheke, at a cost of $3.5 million.

Waiheke businesses faced an average 74% hike in rates charged by the Auckland Regional Council, following the introduction of a business differential. Waiheke High's prom night turned into a nightmare after a serious crash in Onetangi Straight involving the Friends of the Street van, leaving five injured. Mike Lee from Rocky Bay was voted chairman of the Auckland Regional Council. The unpopular speedbumps in Ostend were pinched progressively, leaving Belgium Street smooth once more.

The Police Minister applied successfully for an effective district plan change to build a new Police Station at the entrance of Oneroa.

Flora

To visitors Waiheke means fine, unspoiled beaches, lush vineyards, beautiful native bush reserves, and hill country. Small pockets of mature bush — including trees such as the nikau, taraire, karaka, puriri and areas of raupo swamp — are to be found throughout the eastern half of Waiheke. Much of the rest of the island is undulating farmland and either covered in grass or reverting to scrub, though in some of these places regeneration of native bush is well advanced.

Leaving their signatures everywhere are the crimson flowering pohutukawa providing shade on the coastal beaches, seemingly growing out of solid rock and even found growing at the island's highest elevations; there are the giant macrocarpas (which have become rather an endangered species of late, along with the Norfolk pines); the tall white oleanders in flower, the raupo rushes with brown furry reeds, the blue bells of dyanella, the rare native fushcia (kotukutuku), the blue agapanthus planted along the beach edges, the clumps of white arum lilies, the gardens of daffodils and irises, the clipped hedges of boxhorn and Tacoma, the noxious sweet-smelling yellow ginger plant, seemingly everywhere, and the jonquils growing by the roadside.

The island orchards bear plums, peaches, pears, apples, mulberries, mandarins, grapes, passionfruit, persimmons, figs, walnuts, loquats, grapefruit, tamarillos, kiwifruit, guavas and, off course, the ubiquitous olive.

In spring the roadside freesias still flourish and the native clematis flowers in profuse drifts of white across the tops of the native forests.

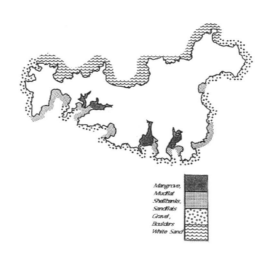

Mangrove,
Mudflat
Shellbanks,
Sandflats
Gravel,
Boulders
White Sand

81

Describing Waiheke vegetation in 1878, Thomas Kirk noted that the old rimu and hardbeech were of great girth, but that the totara and matai were small and scarce. Taraire also was said to be uncommon. Kanuka, however, formed tea-tree forest of "unusual impressiveness". It is certain that this kanuka marked areas where the forest trees had been burnt out by the Maori, either while hunting or maintaining bracken fern as a food plant.

Tawapou still grows by quiet bays where Kirk knew it.

The Waiheke Native Plants Nursery off Onetangi Straight stocks more than 100 different species, the majority sourced and grown from island seed.

The Hauraki Gulf Islands District Plan safeguards all indigenous vegetation and includes standards that must be met when clearing it. All native vegetation higher than three metres is protected.

A reforestation project over 10 years at the McKenzie Reserve will see 1,700 towering pine trees progressively replaced by natives.

There are ecologically significant sites to visit that are listed by the Department of Conservation.

- The Woodlands Bay forest is a rare example of the species diversity once characteristic of the Northland coast.
- The Man O'War Bay forest, extending from sea-level to 200 metres, is the largest on the island and contains kauri, hardbeech, taraire, kohekohe, kahikatea and maire-tawake.
- Te Matuku Bay is the only place in the inner Hauraki Gulf to combine an extensive area of mangroves in near natural condition with an extensive mudflat, a shellbank, and a large area of regenerating native bush.
- Tawaipareira Creek, located by the Refuse Station at Ostend, contains the last remnant of dense cabbage trees.
- The Kuakarau Bay Forest Scenic Reserve on Te Whau Point, occupying the entire western slopes of the Omiha catchment, is a taraire-tawa forest with puriri and kohekohe.
- The 65-hectare Onetangi Reserve owned by the Royal Forest and Bird Protection Society is a taraire-pohutukawa forest with puriri, rewarewa, kohekohe, matai, tawa, kauri and kanuka. It once was part of a large area purchased by the Crown in 1858 which covered much of the northern half of the island, eastwards from Rangihoua Creek.

OPPOSITE: Pohutukawa trees at Palm Beach

- Awaawaroa Bay has a freshwater wetland of raupo and a saline wetland of saltmarsh, saltmeadow and mangrove forest.
- Whakanewha Regional Park has been described as the last remaining complete catchment of prime, possum-free native forest in the inner Hauraki Gulf. The 270-hectare park — the only regional park within Auckland City's boundaries — passed into public ownership in 1993 following a campaign that saved the land from being carved up into lifestyle blocks. It contains two delightful high-tide beaches at Half Moon Bay, and the island's only camping ground. Its major destination is the Cascades track and the small waterfall after which it is named. The old forest is dominated by taraire, kohekohe and nikau, interspersed with species such as tawa, karaka and puriri, as well as pohutukawa by the shore and the occasional rata. Recent growth includes kanuka, mahoe, coprosma and punga. Access is gained from O'Brien Road in Rocky Bay.

ABOVE: Half Moon Bay
OPPOSITE: Roosters at the Onetangi Sports Park

Fauna

At the time of the hoax foot and mouth scare in May 2005, there were a recorded 2,000 cattle, 18,000 sheep, 200 goats and 20 pigs on Waiheke. Twelve major farms and 39 farmers were listed, with the largest livestock numbers at Man O'War Station, followed by Waiheke Station (although only four or five on the list were commercial-sized farms). By way of comparison, Gordon Ingham of *The Settler* wrote in 1952: "The total population of Waiheke is approximately 2,000 people, 24,000 sheep, 2,000 cattle and 13 members of the two roads boards!" At least some things on the island don't change…

In the colonial era the fauna was strictly utilitarian, destined for the dinner plate. Pigeons, wild turkey, wild pork and domestic poultry, and fish and shellfish readily landed from the rocks in the bays, added variety to the menu of early settlers reared on mutton.

In recent times diversification has included an angora goat farm, an alpaca herd, a mussel farm, and oyster farms at Te Matuku Bay, Owhanake Bay and Putiki Bay. Te Matuku Bay Farm alone hopes to harvest up to 100,000 dozen Pacific oysters in the 2005 season.

Geese, rabbits, donkeys and roosters — emblematic of the island's feisty independence movement — are also popular residents.

Ridgeview Farmstay on the Onetangi Straight has farm animals on view, including hens, horses, cats, dogs, goats and pigs.

Almost half of the national snapper catch used to come from the Hauraki Gulf. However, the Ministry of Fisheries introduced a quota system for commercial fishing in 1986. Nowadays the recreational fisherman can realistically hope to catch a flounder, trevally, snapper, kahawai, kingfish, red moki, red gurnard or red cod. In spite of the Ministry's bag quota, the reality is that perhaps now very few of recreational fishermen are catching 20 fish or more in a day; most bring home two or three fish if they're lucky.

Dolphins are a relatively common sight around the shores during winter and spring, and orca, too — known for taking penguins off the rocks.

Te Matuku Bay is Waiheke's foremost haven for both rare and migrant birds. As a nesting colony for rare bird species this bay is probably unsurpassed elsewhere in the region.

The island is home to an almost *Who's Who* of the bird world — the threatened reef heron, the banded rail, the New Zealand dotterel, the banded dotterel and the black shag, brown quail, brown teal, Californian quail, the gannet, Caspian tern, fantail, fernbird, grey duck, grey-faced petrel, grey warbler, grey teal, kaka, kingfisher, little black shag, little blue penguin, little shag, mallard, morepork, godwhit, wood pigeon, paradise shelduck, pied shag, pied stilt, pipit, reef heron, rosella, sharp-tailed sandpiper, skua, skylark, South Island oystercatcher, tui, turnstone, white-faced heron, white-fronted heron, white-fronted tern, wrybill, the variable oystercatcher *et al*. Not to mention the majestic hawks hanging over the valleys, or the unpopular, aggressive mynahs.

In the east of the island, raupo swamp is the natural habitat and breeding ground for pukeko, bittern and the spotless crake. There is also an unusual breeding colony of the relatively rare spotted shag at Anita Bay.

There are hopes that bellbirds — which have been extinct in the Auckland region since the 1860s — may make a reappearance, following a sighting on Rakino Island after a rat eradication campaign. It is hoped that their next stop will be Church Bay…

ABOVE: A kereru in a kowhai tree
OPPOSITE: Te Matuku Bay

Marine Reserves

Te Matuku Bay has become the fourth marine reserve in the Auckland region (after Long Bay, Pollen Island and Goat Island near Leigh); New Zealand as a whole has 27 marine reserves. The 690-hectare reserve on Waiheke includes areas of saltmarsh and mangroves, large inter-tidal mudflats, superb shellbanks, and — in the deeper water — beds of horse mussels, large seaweeds and crayfish habitats.

The reserve includes Whites Bay to the west, but not Orapiu to the east. It stretches out to Passage Rock in the channel and over to Ponui Island's Kauri Point.

The Department of Conservation identified Te Matuku Bay as an area of national significance, in part due to the rare and endangered marine bird species that feed and nest there. It is also an important area for marine wildlife with snapper, kingfish and trevally. It is hoped that an increase in marine and bird life will attract divers and visitors — as at Goat Island, which draws about 200,000 visitors a year.

Noteworthy are the vegetation sequences of the inter-tidal area. They provide the saline flora component to an unbroken sequence

from currently protected upland forest to freshwater and saline wetlands. The mangroves and estuarine waters of the bay are part of the extremely productive, coastal foodchain.

The reserve skirts around a seven-hectare oyster farm which cultivates Pacific oysters. It is probably the only oyster farm in such a position in the world — a happy meeting because, as filter feeders, oysters are very much a reflection of the quality of the water in which they live.

An area between Hakaimango Point and Thompsons Point on the northern coast has also long been identified for possible marine reserve status, encompassing a core area, which would be totally protected, and a buffer zone where some activities would be permitted.

The north-east coastline is rugged, with rocky bluffs, wave-cut platforms, reefs, stacks, pinnacles and islands, and the occasional sandy bay. These provide for a variety of reef fish species.

It has been suggested that the core area — incorporating Hekerua, Sandy, Enclosure and Repo bays, Big and Little Palm Beach and Nani Island — would have a total ban on all types of fishing. Within the area is a recognised snapper feeding ground and a fossil beach dating back to the Lower Miocene Age some 19 million years ago.

The combination of a rich and varied marine fauna (fish, shellfish and birds), together with the spectacular scenery of the coastline and islands, as well as the interesting and unusual submarine landforms, make a compelling case for another marine reserve.

ABOVE: Wetland at the head of Putiki Bay

Walkways

There is a network of walkways and undulating tracks one can follow to quietly explore the island away from the increasingly busy roads. Auckland City's walkway brochure is worth picking up from the visitor office (either at Matiatia wharf or Artworks), listing the favourite walks on the island which allow visitors to meander through an island heritage of pristine bush, sandy coves, farmland and reserve.

Waiheke has a host of walkways to choose from, partly due to provisions being made back at the early subdivision stage of the island's development. Since then, input from the Waiheke Visitor Information Board, investment of Waiheke Community Board SLIPS (small local improvement projects) money — combined with local initiatives and enthusiasm — has resulted in a diverse range of bush, coastal and rural walkways for the enjoyment of all.

Rewarding walks for those with limited time on Waiheke include:

- The loop from Matiatia around the north-western tip of the island to Owhanake Bay, where you can enjoy coastal vistas, glimpse local vineyards and enjoy beaches.
- The Church Bay circuit, complete with an architectural wonderland of no-expense spared, designer homes.
- The Royal Forest and Bird Protection Society's bush reserve off Waiheke Road, Onetangi. The full circuit takes about 90 minutes, but the small circular walk takes about 15 minutes.
- The Orapiu, Hunterville, Pearl Bay and Te Matuku Bay loop, which takes about one hour return.
- The steep climb from Little Oneroa Beach up the cliffside to McIntosh Road, Newton Road and then on to explore the north-facing bays.
- The walk from the top of Goodwin Avenue and Queens Drive down to Watters Glen and Hekerua Bay, and then up the Te Aroha Avenue incline to Karaka Road and on to Palm Beach (Don's Track).
- The Waikopou Bay walkway (Mac's Track).
- The coastal, unsealed road between Blackpool and Surfdale.

- The three-kilometre, 40-minute coastal walk from Kuakarau Bay to Te Whau Drive, traversing coastal reserve. It is a stunning landscape of native bush and seaviews, and includes a Pa site.
- At the southern end of Esslin Road is a reserve and informal tracks leading to the beach.
- The extraordinary coastal bush of Whakanewha Regional Park.
- The Onetangi to Palm Beach Ballysaggart walkway (Thompson's Track).
- The Atawai Whenua Forest and Bird Reserve on the hillside to the south of Matiatia.

The road to Stony Batter

Stony Batter

T he Japanese attack on Pearl Harbour on December 7, 1941
and the spread of war to the Pacific created fears of invasion.
Among the defences erected were three gun emplacements
at Stony Batter.

There, near the north-west tip of Waiheke, huge andecite
boulders lie like giant marbles deposited over the landscape by
volcanic activity some eight million years ago. Debate continues
over the volcanic source which threw the boulders on to this
Waiheke site — the eruption which created Lake Pupuke in
Takapuna, an undersea volcano in the Gulf or another one near
Thames, are the three contenders.

Two hundred men arrived in October, 1942 to build the concrete
labyrinth which first required the construction of a wharf at Man
O'War Bay and a metal road up to the site.

Stony Batter (batter is 'receding slope') comprised 914 metres
of tunnels and stairways, a magazine chamber, plotting room,
engine room and three oil stores — all to feed three, huge 9.2 inch
guns with 10-metre barrels capable of firing two 172kg shells a
minute, 45 kilometres over the horizon, or at inland targets from
Wellsford to Te Kauwhata. The guns were mounted on large rollers
and could rotate 360 degrees and elevate to 35 degrees. The tunnels,
living quarters and storage rooms were completed in 1944, although
local folklore has it that construction was finished on Armistice
Day, 1945.

The giant guns of British naval design were only fired once, to
see if they worked, and were obsolete by the end of the war. In
1962 they were sold to an Australian scrap merchant who cut them
up and on sold the metal, ironically, to the Japanese.

The site formed part of the coastal defence system for the
Auckland region in addition to those established on North Head,
Motutapu and Rangitoto islands. It was held for defence purposes
until 1968, when it was declared surplus to requirements and
became Crown land.

On November 5, 1982 there was an inspection by the Minister
of Lands, Mr Elworthy, of the Crown land comprising 18.4 hectares
taken compulsorily in 1942 under the Defence Emergency
Regulations. It was stated that the area had important historic

features which should not be passed into private ownership.

Pulp and paper magnate John Spencer — whose land stretches from half of Wairua (Carey) Bay all around the north-east tip down to include Wairere Bay — attempted to persuade the Crown to sell him the 98 acres at the centre of his 4,450-acre property, and he placed a locked gate across the access road. The legal battle with Mr Spencer over possession of roads through his farmland around Stony Batter began in 1983, and was resolved — against him — nearly 20 years later.

It now takes 15-minutes to reach the fortification via a public walkway from the carpark, though an easement on Mr Spencer's property. The Stony Batter Protection and Restoration Society is the driving force behind the restoration of the tunnels and complex, which is classified and protected under the Historic Places Trust.

Stony Batter is a must-see for its historical significance, the feat of engineering and the dramatic location. A concrete bunker houses a pictorial display of its military history and the role it played in Auckland's coastal defence. It attracts some 50,000 visitors annually. Concession charges were approved in 2004.

ABOVE: Owhiti Bay
PREVIOUS PAGE: Huge andecite boulders at Stony Batter

Economy

The fortunes of the island can be simply illustrated by over 100 years of boat traffic through the Waiheke Channel — from Northern Company steamers and shingle-loaded scows to the present day catamaran ferries, yachts and pleasure boats.

The traditional resources of the island economy were forestry, fishing, farming and small-scale mining; and, even before 1900, Waiheke was seen as an excursion destination. Nowadays, the shift to marine suburb and small-scale urbanisation has seen an associated rise in retailing and service jobs, tourism, arts, craft and cottage industries, the increasing importance of wine and olives, and an ever-growing number of islanders (plus laptops and mobiles) commuting to work in the city. By 2005, up to 1,000 commuters were making the daily return trip to Auckland.

The 3,000-acre block covering part of the Puke range of hill country in the east, carrying Hereford cattle and Perrendale sheep, is perhaps the largest example of mixed dairy farming. Meanwhile, Green awareness has seen a few permaculture operations established on organic principles, like Mike Delamore's Fossil Bay Farm and the Eco-Village at Awaawaroa Bay.

The island's long love affair with alternative lifestylers has seen the formation of a credit union dedicated to not making a profit, and various labour/barter arrangements where goods and services are supplied for 'green dollars' — units of exchange allowing A to provide B with goods or a service and vice-versa, with no money changing hands. This innovation has been subverted in the city by unscrupulous wheeler-dealers into a bottomless, black economy where the IRD is deprived of GST; but on Waiheke, the element of community help and reliance is still pertinent.

ABOVE: The former Rothschilds' estate at Putiki Bay

Building (and associated trades) is a traditional industry on Waiheke, involving a large number of the population. The post-war fibrolite bach has been succeeded by more substantial board-and-batten or weatherboard homes, pole houses, modulock or pre-built homes, and architecturally designed homes of glass and steel clad with cedar, other hardwoods or cement plaster. Adobe and mudbrick are also popular, with many structures on the island now being permanent monuments to mudbrick pioneer Vince Ogletree, who died in 2005. Mr Ogletree created structures ranging from handcrafted chalet-style homes, million dollar houses, down to café garden walls and pony club jumps.

Over-fishing of the Hauraki Gulf has seen a decline in the local fishing industry. This has, however, not affected the number of anglers sports-fishing, and the slack has been taken up by fishing and launch charter operators.

The beauty, peace and tranquillity of Waiheke has always encouraged artistic creativity and the island remains home to many artists.

Another huge industry on the island is real estate. Coastal land close to the city has become so prized that prices have escalated beyond many people's wildest dreams. Property prices doubled between 2000 and 2003; from 1998 to 2004 prices jumped 71% in the Hauraki Gulf islands, and it was Waiheke which led the way. There are now six major real estate agencies in Oneroa, and a conservative estimate of over 50 practising real estate agents on the island. The sheer volume of real estate advertising every week — in the letterbox, on the ferry, in the local newspapers — beggars belief.

Apart from tourism though, THE growth industry — and Waiheke's future economically-speaking — could lie with winemaking. Some of the best vineyards in the country have been planted on the island over the past two decades, and their success makes it likely that more will surely follow.

Other horticultural activities of note include orchards, market gardens, orchids, tree and shrub nurseries, and beekeeping.

Everyone agrees that water is the key element affecting future sustainable growth on the island.

PREVIOUS PAGE: Stonyridge Vineyard

Winemaking

The island's maritime climate results in higher levels of grape sugar and fruit intensity than vineyards on the isthmus. The factors of low rainfall, warm temperatures, less humidity and more sunshine than Auckland, along with sea protection from severe drought and flooding, allow Waiheke grapes to produce a near perfect alcohol level, fruitiness, ph and acidity levels, achieved moreover in the natural conditions of the vineyards and not by chemistry in the stainless steel vats.

The viticulture of Waiheke wineries involve no insecticides and minimal use of accepted fungicides.

The beginnings of winemaking on Waiheke were inauspicious. A Yugoslav family, the Gradiskas, using hybrid grapes to make fortified wines, saw their early venture end in tragedy in the 1950s with the grandfather killed on a tractor, and another family member committing suicide. They had carved a seven-acre vineyard out of swampy land in Seaview Road in the 1930s, and their product — known locally as 'Purple Death' — came in flagons; it was said that the equivalent of one bottle rendered one senseless, if not unconscious.

In the late 1970s Kim and Jeannette Goldwater established cabernet sauvignon stock on their estate above Ostend Causeway, in spite of the Rural Bank's refusal to give them a loan. In 2001 the pioneering Goldwater Estate was named as one of only two New Zealand vineyards listed by *Wines and Spirits* as among the world's best.

In 1982 they were followed by Stephen White, a young horticulturist who began the labour-intensive task of planting his Stonyridge Vineyard while holding down a Monday to Friday job in Auckland. He had studied in Bordeaux and Italy, and had crewed in the first Whitbread round-the-world yacht race, hopping off in

ABOVE: Awaawaroa Bay Vineyard

South America to work in Chilean vineyards, and then California. He planted cabernet sauvignon, merlot, malbec and cabernet franc grapes on five acres at Stonyridge.

White's vineyard is overlooked by an olive grove. It is nestled beside a 100-metre high rocky ridge called Stonyridge, in poor but free-draining soil (deep, stony clay rich in manganese) one kilometre from the sea. The winery is of European design (French Chateau), with three, level process areas and an underground barrel cellar. All wines are gently aged in oak barriques and are not filtered before bottling.

Doug and Anne Hamilton established Peninsula Estate Vineyard above Oneroa Bay in 1986, and in the 1990s there was a subsequent explosion of vineyards across the island with a great diversity of grape varieties, white and red. It also saw the formation of the Waiheke Wine Growers' Association.

By 2003 some 26 vineyards had been established, containing around 300,000 vines. They produced 227 tonnes of red and 42 tonnes of white grapes, which grew in 2004 to approximately 448 tonnes of red and 118 tonnes of white.

The accent on small is beautiful has seen Waiheke vineyards planted and operated to yield low quantities of extremely high quality fruit. They regularly harvest cabernet sauvignon earlier and riper than any other viticultural area in New Zealand.

There are at least 27 different Waiheke vines, including bordeaux blends, merlot, cabernet sauvignon, pinot noir, malbec, sauvignon blanc, syrah, chardonnay and viognier.

Cable Bay has some 24 hectares of vineyards on 10 sites, making it potentially the second largest producer after John Spencer's Stony Batter Estate.

It is said that Te Whau Vineyard boasts the most extensive wine list in the country, with more than 500 varieties in the cellar. The emphasis is on New Zealand, French and Australian.

ABOVE: Putiki Bay Vineyard
OPPOSITE: Passage Rock Vineyard

The inaugural Waiheke Island Wine Festival attracted over 4,000 wine lovers from around the world in February 2003, and is now held annually at seven of the most well-known vineyards, although there is talk of confining it to just one site.

The latest estimate had Waiheke's winegrowing industry investing approximately $7.5 million into the island's economy in 2004. The vineyards purchased $10 million in goods and services from other businesses, with 75% staying on Waiheke. The winegrowers racked up revenues of $11.3 million with 43% coming from wine made from Waiheke grapes, and 32% from other operations such as restaurants, tours and accommodation. The industry employs more than 100 permanent staff full-time and more than 350 seasonal staff, and attracted an estimated 185,000 visitors to the island in 2004.

There is, however, a natural limit to vineyard growth — the availability of suitable land and sufficient water, and the escalating cost of land are important factors.

A misty winter scene at Peninsula Estate Vineyard

Olive Oil

There is no doubt about it: Waiheke's olive oil is among the best in the world. In 2003 the island's fledgling olive oil industry was put firmly on the international stage after judges at the prestigious Los Angeles County Fair awarded Waiheke oils three of New Zealand's four gold medals, when 176 different olive oils, from 113 producers, were judged. Rangihoua Estate took two of the golds with oils blended from the island's oldest commercial grove at Stonyridge Vineyard (planted in 1982).

Waiheke's edge is that its microclimates produce early ripening fruit, which means the oils can be on the market one month ahead of the rest of New Zealand. The stony subsoil also makes Waiheke good for olives. And the climate of breezes and heavy winds reduce the number of pests affecting the trees. It has also helped that the rainfall has so far fallen at the right time.

The numbers are sketchy but there are at least 50 olive groves on the island at present, and an estimated 30,000 trees. The olive tree has also become a *de rigeur* planting for homeowners seeking some Mediterranean ambience on their properties; so its popularity seems assured.

Once a tree gets to 12-years old, it can produce 100kgs of fruit. The first stone mill for olives in New Zealand was brought to the island in 2001. It can process 150 kilos of olives per hour. Rangihoua Estate has the largest oil processor in the Auckland region, imported from Florence, with a capacity of 500 kilos an hour.

Most of Waiheke's olive oil produce is sold within the Auckland region.

ABOVE: A newly planted olive grove at Oneroa

Transport

Nowadays, 35 minutes from downtown Auckland by fast, modern catamaran ferry — with full bar and catering service — makes the island an ideal day trip or an idyllic holiday spot. Fullers run up to 20 return sailings daily, between 5.45am and 11.45pm, and it's virtually an every hour service.

Subritzky Sealink vehicular ferries provide an hourly link to the island, sailing between Half Moon Bay, Panmure, and Kennedy Point seven days a week. There is also a car ferry service operating from the Western Viaduct near Wynyard Wharf, Downtown.

There is a twice-weekly, two hour fast ferry service between Auckland and Coromandel via Orapiu, leaving Wednesday and Sunday, by Kawau Kat Cruises.

Small planes make taxi flights from the Waiheke Airfield (*aka* the Reeve Airfield) at the top of Trig Hill Road, and helicopter flights from Mechanics Bay are available for charter.

On Waiheke, buses meet all ferry sailings and alternative transport is provided by taxis, rental cars, shuttle buses and vans, jeeps, mini-buses, motorbikes, scooters, motor-assisted cycles, mountain bikes and horses.

Out on the water, sea kayaks, windsurfers, catamarans and dinghies are available for hire in summer.

It's all a far cry from a not so distant yesteryear, for the story of transport to and from the island has been a drawn-out and troublesome affair — a litany of public hearings, bitter debate, personal acrimony and suspended judgements. However, with the advent of a reliable fast service in 1987, all that has become just a bad but colourful memory.

For until then, passengers made the sea crossing between Waiheke and Auckland in one boat from the previous century (the *Baroona*, built in 1898 for a New South Wales sheep station manager and named after his station), and two converted Fairmile naval patrol launches from the Second World War (the *Iris Moana* and the *Motonui*). The trip by historical vessel took 80 minutes, and motor launches were used to back-up a licensed service monopoly.

PRECEDING PAGE: Matiatia Bay
OPPOSITE: The Baroona

Looking back, the earliest record is of the steamship *Transit* making twice-weekly visits to the island in 1887.

By 1927 Ostend was the main port of call. The fare was two shillings and sixpence return.

In 1936, eastern Waiheke and Ponui settlers clubbed together to start the Waiheke Passenger Service Ltd., and the *Baroona* (also known affectionately as 'the Galloping Ghost') was purchased. Originally built as a trawler, the *Baroona* ran from Auckland up the Waiheke Channel calling in at Rocky Bay, Awaawaroa, Orapiu, Cowes, Ponui and, when necessary, Man O'War Bay.

Since then the *Baroona* (renamed *Captain Hook's Jolly Roger*) has surreally metamorphosised into a themed restaurant based on *Peter Pan* in Manukau.

Its original funnel, however, is on display at the Waiheke Island Brewery, makers of *Baroona* beer, at the Onetangi Road Vineyard.

"Why not a State shipping service?" the *Waiheke Resident* asked on the front page of the April 20, 1949 edition. On the island at the time Dr Warren was selling his Model A Ford, Oneroa Pictures were screening every Wednesday at the Ascot Theatre, Lofty Blomfield was running the Oneroa dances, Bub Smith and his band were headlining at the Palm Beach Hall dance, the Anzac Day parade at Ostend realised 10 pounds in spite of a shortage of poppies (only 200 poppies were available), a pair of work boots cost 25 shillings, and there were daily ferry boat sailings from Kings Wharf to Oneroa, Surfdale, Palm Beach, Ostend, Onetangi, Orapiu, Omiha, Connells Bay, Cowes Bay and Ponui.

In 1954 the Waiheke Shipping Company began a regular service to Matiatia.

An amphibian seaplane service, started by Fred Ladd in 1955, landed in Surfdale and operated on and off for 30 years until the antiquity of the 'Sea Bees' and the arrival of the fast ferry service combined to make a regular service uneconomic.

The ill-fated hydrofoil *Manu-Wai* operated a fast 25-minute link with the mainland from 1967 until 1973. It carried 73 passengers and the fare was 15 shillings return (the slow ferry fare was 10 shillings return at the time). In December 1973, a proposed new

manning scale led the Seamen's Union to place a black ban on the vessel. For a decade the *Manu-Wai* rusted on the hard at Mechanics Bay before it was sold off. It later made a brief reappearance in the Gulf flying the flag of Dominion Breweries.

Until the opening of the new Princes Wharf terminal in 2005, Waiheke travellers were subjected to third-world facilities at the Auckland end. The shelter was a converted shipping container. Previous to that was a shelter opened in 1976 that seated 46 people. Leo Dromgoole, unpopular owner of the Waiheke Shipping Company from 1968 to 1981, said in opposing the shelter at the time that it would become "a sleep-out for drunks".

Another long-running saga has involved Fullers' dumping of

raw sewage into the inner Hauraki Gulf. This ceased finally in March 2005 — 10 years after reaching an agreement in principle to share the cost of a sewage pump-out downtown. The ratepayer-funded facility at the downtown ferry terminal cost $400,000.

A hovermarine service operated fitfully from March 1978, but the second-hand *Wakatere* (formerly the *Blue Dolphin* from Tasmania) was plagued by mechanical problems and the service — lacking a fast back-up — was withdrawn after a few months.

The ferries were taken over by the Hudson family in August 1981, and the much-loved *Quickcat* — built in Perth and capable of carrying 650 passengers — began plying the run in 1987. Trading as Gulf Ferries, the company merged with Fullers in 1988. The *Jet Raider* — a fast, mono-hull 400-passenger vessel built in Fremantle, Western Australia — arrived in July 1990.

Pacifica Shipping ran in competition to Gulf Ferries over the 1991/2 summer but then withdrew, having managed to attract, at best, a 10% share of passenger loadings.

Auckland City and Downer and Company opened a new $2.3 million wharf at Matiatia in May 1993.

The *Iris Moana* — which launched the worker service in 1948 — headed off to a new life in South-East Asia in 1994.

Fullers' Gulf Ferries fleet was further enlarged in the 1990s by the addition of two smaller catamaran ferries and a large one, the *Superflyte*, which arrived in 1997.

Pacific Ferries ran a cut-price, one-hour service over the summer of 1998, with the *Lady Wakehurst* holding 700 passengers, but then withdrew.

George Hudson was honoured as an Officer of the New Zealand Order of Merit in 2000, after turning an ageing ferry fleet into the Gulf's modern commuter and tourism enterprise.

Subritzky added the $6 million twin-hulled *MV Seacat* — carrying up to 55 cars and 500 passengers — to its fleet in 2003. A year later it was bought out by South Australia's largest private tourism operator, Kangaroo Island Sealink.

In February 2004, Auckland City opened its new $3.2 million wharf terminal at Matiatia.

Meanwhile, a 170-metre breakwater and recreational boat ramp was approved for Kennedy Point. Currently being built, it is to give protection for vehicular ferries and their passengers as they enter and leave the port; the cost: $2.5 million.

Last but not least, mention must be made of little Hannah Urquhart-Greaves (3.7kg), who made her entry into the world in 2004 inside the toilet compartment of the *Quickcat*. She is believed to be the first baby ever born on the Waiheke run.

PRECEDING PAGE: Today's fast catamaran ferries provide a shuttle-service between the island and Auckland City

OPPOSITE: The hydrofoil Manu-Wai
TOP: Fullers' old waiting-room on the city wharf
ABOVE: With only five return sailings a day, missing the boat in the late 1970s meant, literally, throwing a sickie...
OVERLEAF: Kennedy Point

Tourism

The 1,850 square miles of the Hauraki Gulf provide a playground of islands for Aucklanders, at their front door. It is home to over 100,000 boats, of which 2,000 have moorings on Waiheke.

Waiheke — the largest of the Gulf islands — offers the visitor a laid-back interlude or lifestyle with a great choice of recreational pursuits including boating, bowling, fishing, golf, horse-riding, mini-golf, swimming, surfing, diving, tennis, tramping, windsurfing or just lazing in the sun with a good book or magazine. At present, an estimated 65% of people coming to stay on the island are from Auckland; 15% are from other parts of New Zealand and 20% are from overseas.

There is a wide range of restaurants, bars and cafés to enjoy, and accommodation ranges from the budget to the luxurious — from simple beach houses, backpackers, bed and breakfast homestays to internationally accredited private hotels. Renting accommodation on the island has become more popular, in line with the internet explosion; at the last count, a web search showed almost 200 listings. The only camping ground is at the Whakanewha Reserve, and there is a youth hostel at Onetangi.

There are bowling clubs at Oneroa and Surfdale, tennis courts at Onetangi, Ostend and Rocky Bay, and two riding schools for those wishing to explore the island on horseback. Newer activities have added a paintball adventure challenge (using non-stain vegetable dyes), a frisbee-throwing course, paragliding, skydiving, a mixed gym and a ladies' gym, and a skate park on reclaimed land at Tawaipareira Creek, Ostend. A new $1.9 million recreation centre at the Waiheke High School opened in 2003, greatly improving options for indoor sport on the island, and an indoor heated swimming pool is planned on the lower field off Donald Bruce Road, at a cost of $5 million.

The 120-acre council reserve adjacent to Onetangi Straight is used by the Waiheke Country Club, which has laid out an 18-hole golf course open to the public. The golf course is really nine holes, but

PRECEDING PAGE: Holiday makers and cows seeking shade at Cactus Bay
OPPOSITE: Sculpture on the Gulf — 'Hauraki' / Paul Dibble

has two tees on each fairway so you can go around twice. There are plans for a back nine. Beyond the golf club is the 50-hectare sports park, scene of particularly frenetic activity at weekends.

The Waiheke Historical Society also has its museum and historic village along the straight, including an old woolshed which dates back to the 1870s, and two restored cottages where time has stood still. The museum includes photographs of early settlement and a comprehensive collection of artifacts, and gives a good idea of what the life of Waiheke pioneers was all about.

The 1,600 square-metre site housing Artworks at the gateway of Oneroa village is an arts centre complete with library, theatre, cinema, art gallery, Beach Radio 99.4FM, shops, Indian restaurant and Tourism Auckland's visitor centre. It also houses Whittaker's Musical Museum — an interactive space with regular performances and a unique collection of musical instruments gathered from around the world, dating back as far as the 16th Century, including the country's oldest Steinway grand piano. Sunday markets are held in the courtyard at Artworks during the summer months.

ABOVE: Greg Johnson playing at the Stonyridge Verandah Café
PRECEDING PAGE: The Mudbrick Vineyard

122

Other art galleries include the Rockit Gallery and the Red Shed, both dedicated to Waiheke art, and the Green Gallery at Palm Beach. There is a proliferation of tours on offer — including vineyard tours, island discovery tours, Stony Batter, an artist studio tour, even a tour by Harley Davidson.

There are two dedicated sculpture parks on the island at Te Whau Point and Connells Bay, plus the award-winning biennial Sculpture on the Gulf — the nation's premier award for sculptors, offering a top prize of $10,000 — along the Church Bay walkway above Matiatia, which is held over two weeks in summer.

ABOVE: The 'Big Dig' at the Onetangi beach races
OVERLEAF: Palm Beach from Tiri View Road

Real Estate

Waiheke Island is very different from the rustic community of only 30 years ago. Then, you could buy a family home on a good section for as little as $6,000 — the same house in 2005 would probably set you back at least half a million dollars!

The lid on island real estate really came off in the late 1980s when a regular, fast ferry service put Queen Street only 35 minutes and a beer or glass of wine away. The corresponding explosion in computer technology, capped by the internet in the late 1990s, suddenly allowed many more people to work away from the confines of office life. Auckland's ever-worsening transport gridlock also helped to make Waiheke an attractive proposition for people who valued lifestyle on a par with income; as did the global feeding frenzy on coastal land post-Millennium, and state-of-the-art marketing *par excellence*.

People with income were welcomed by lifestyle subdivisions such as occurred at Church Bay, Matiatia Estates, at Te Whau and, most recently, at the 130-hectare, 34-lot Park Point development. Fantasy designer homes were created with no-expense-spared fittings and, in places, private roads and locked gates. The building sector boomed and although there are some conspicuous failures, many beautiful homes have been created and magnificently landscaped. The vista is becoming definitely Mediterranean, but you are just as likely to find, say, a French farmhouse, as you are a design borrowed from Cape Cod or Arizona.

Recently, a six-member building advisory panel, approved by the Auckland City Council, has been set-up to assess and advise on building design and development within the Hauraki Gulf. Developers are being encouraged to discuss their proposals with the panel as early as possible, pre-application, free-of-charge.

There is ambiguity as to where the 'visual impact' of a building on a ridgeline is to be viewed. Nominally, permitted activity allows a building to be built on or above a ridgeline by eight metres.

ABOVE: 'Reflect your success... and express your excess!'

Some milestones and landmarks in Waiheke building and real estate include:-

• The Glenora Estate Vineyard, incorporating a 17th Century-style Brittany farmhouse *(ABOVE)* with olive groves and a luxury hospitality business. Situated on eight acres of paddock and 800 square metres of vineyard and maturing olive grove, protected by lavender and native bush. The building materials were obtained from around the world; including Indian sandstone, Italian marble tiles, French zinc panelling for the kitchen, handcrafted window furniture from England, rustic beams from Australia, and hand-laminated oak beams from the United States. *Monument Historique* glazed terracotta roofing tiles were imported from France to give the house its 'thatched cottage' look — the only roof of its kind in New Zealand. Everything being made as authentic as possible — from genuine flagstones to the solid oak doors put together with hand-forged nails. Complete with panoramic views of the sea and a private walkway to nearby Te Miro Cave.

- The 13.9-hectare Lyttle property — also known as Te Rere Cove *(ABOVE)* — with house, vineyard and olive grove, sold for an undisclosed sum over $5 million; a record price for a residential life-block. The property was bought in 1992 when Church Bay was subdivided and a hectare of grapes and 10 acres of olive trees were planted.

- The Cowes Bay beachfront property — a 35-hectare farm with its own wharf (complete with band rotunda), tennis courts, indoor pool and a 1,200 square-metre mansion with nine bedrooms and five bathrooms, a two-bedroom caretaker's cottage, three separate studios, a wine cellar, boatshed and woolshed. Its Irish owner put the property up for sale for $26 million.

- The Glass House in Rocky Bay, designed as a unique form of boutique accommodation and voted one of the top 101 hotels in the world.

- New Zealand billionaire Graeme Hart purchased a 40-hectare block at Church Bay for a price believed to be $15 million.

• The Lewenz adobe home at Church Bay *(ABOVE)* — with a terracotta-tiled roof, courtyards, solar panels, lavender gardens, high dormer windows and art studio — was built from adobes made of local quarry mix: 15 percent clay, the rest sand and aggregate, pioneered on Waiheke by earth building contractor Vince Ogletree.

Adobe fitted Gabrielle and Claude's design brief, being a material that is abundant, available, cheap and local.

They have created an adobe home that reflects their diverse backgrounds in Europe and America, and as a demonstration model and testing place for their ideas. It timelessly recalls Santa Fe, Tuscany and Provence on a Waiheke Island hillside, and is reputedly the largest earthbrick house in New Zealand.

OVERLEAF: The boatsheds at Rocky Bay

Island Life

The island is host to a myriad assortment of annual events which reflect its diverse community. Perhaps the most popular, colourful and enduring are the beach races.

The Onetangi beach horse races are an island tradition, beginning in 1883, and are usually held in late summer. At their inception the races were considered an opportunity by local farmers and Maori to pit their riding skills against one another, with well-known pioneer families — including the Hooks, the Browns, the Gordons and the Days — taking part. Riding side-saddle to win the 1912 Ladies' Race was Mrs Day, the hem of her dress weighed down, for the sake of propriety, with pennies.

By 1924 the races had grown so big that regular horses and punters, attracted from Auckland by the large stakes, were accompanied on the morning boat by Police, who shut the races down because of 'excessive gambling'.

The race tradition was revived in 1983 by the Waiheke Historical Society, who ran the event for 10 years before a further lapse until 1998 when the Rotary Club of Waiheke took it over as a major community fundraiser — in 2004, $26,000 was raised. It is now a huge family day on the beach with heaps of prizes and competitions.

There is an annual garden party fundraiser on behalf of the island's hospice support services. In 2004 this party raised a record $80,000.

The annual half-marathon Wharf to Wharf Fun Run — from Orapiu to Matiatia — in January attracts hundreds, and takes around 90 minutes for the leaders to complete. It is regarded as the toughest 25-kilometre run in the country because of the hilly terrain, which takes in Mount Maunganui, and it is the traditional training event for the Rotorua Marathon. There is also an alternative shorter course of 12 kilometres from Onetangi to Matiatia

The Waiheke Easter Jazz Festival draws thousands of visitors to the island. The brainchild of island identity and Connecticut-born jazz musician David Paquette, it started small in 1991 with one man, a piano and a good idea, and grew ever larger. There was

ABOVE: Onetangi beach races
LEFT: Third place in the sandcastle competition
OVERLEAF: Willow Flare — the best dressed in the field

a hiatus in 2005, and a return to a more intimate festival is planned for 2006.

Other shows include Guy Fawkes at the Dirt-track; 'Fashion Addiction', featuring Waiheke's clothes designers; a Kindergarden casino night fundraiser; a surfcasting competition at Onetangi Beach; an annual wine festival; the 'hookers' ball'; a trolley derby down Ocean View Road; a Christmas Parade; a storytelling festival; a garden 'safari'; and a 'Junk to Funk' recycling fashion extravaganza highlighting materials gathered from the waste stream

On the subject of waste, Waiheke has a proud record (none finer in Auckland) — in line with the old saying about judging a community by what it throws away. Recyclable tins, plastics, aluminium cans, bottles and glass, paper and cardboard are sorted and separated into plastic shopping bags at source and left out at the gate with the official red rubbish bag on collection day (Monday or Tuesday) once a week. A local community development company, Clean Stream, then takes it to the transfer station at Ostend, and subsequent sorting reduces the waste going to Auckland landfills.

In the first year of operation, landfill was reduced by 1,000 tonnes (it cost $200 per tonne to go to Auckland), and recycling was increased by 345% — creating one dozen jobs in the process.

Less than half of the waste picked up is now going on the barge to the Auckland landfill, and with recycling up to 1,400 tonnes per year and the cost of landfill up to $230 a tonne, savings are running at $700,000 a year. Some 19 people are employed on rubbish collection days.

Island street names tell their own stories about island life. Ostend and Belgium Street marked worldwide sympathy for Belgium when it was invaded by Germany in the First World War; Oscar Natske, who left the island to become a world famous opera singer, is also remembered with a street name in Ostend.

One enduring modern institution is the island's oldest weekly newspaper, *Gulf News*, which celebrated its 30th birthday in 2003 by going full colour.

TOP: David Paquette (left) at the Waiheke Jazz Festival
BOTTOM: Sunday stockcar racing at the foot of Rocky Bay hill

The island's new found prosperity and transformation into 'hot property' has been witnessed by the advent of two further weekly publications in the past decade — the *Waiheke Marketplace* and the *Waiheke Week*. Both are give-aways and a guaranteed good read.

Cars are banned from all beaches, except for embarking or retrieving boats; all fires require a permit; and dogs and horses are not allowed on beaches from 9am to 4pm from Labour Weekend though to Easter. The restriction is extended to 6pm between December 24 and February 1.

ABOVE: It's always Thanksgiving Day on Waiheke...

Directory

Useful phone numbers on Waiheke Island.

111 Fire/Police/Ambulance
372 5222 Animal Emergency
372 8484 Vet
303 1303 Coastguard
372 8576 Red Cross Medical Surgery
379 4240 Auckland Police
372 1150 Waiheke Police
372 8824 Piritahi Hau Ora Trust
372 5005 Ostend Medical Centre
372 8473 Oneroa Fire Station
372 8666 Onetangi Fire Station
379 2020 Noise Control
0800 10 18 10 Power Lines
379 4240 Search and Rescue
372 6849 Oneroa Dental Surgery
372 7422 Waiheke Dental Centre
372 5245/372 8312 Pharmacies

372 8977/372 5316 Water Delivery
372 5000 Waiheke Air
372 9777/372 8038 Taxi
372 8876/372 8949/372 8661 Petrol
372 9914/372 1018/372 8998/372 8635 Rental Cars
367 9119 Fullers Infophone
300 5900 Subritzky Car Ferry
534 5990 Waiheke Shipping Car Ferry
372 4240 Cinema
372 9907 Art Gallery
360 0750 Animal Control
372 5222 SPCA
374 1325 Library
372 5099 Auckland City Service Centre/Waiheke
372 1234 Visitor Information Centre
372 9193 Nightowls
372 8640 Citizens' Advice Bureau

Photo Credits

Pages 32, 84, 144 © Vivienne Picard
Pages 14, 22 © AA Tourism
Pages 28, 66, 76 © Auckland Public Library
Pages 18, 19, 60, 64, 67, 71 © Auckland Museum

Pages 4, 26, 34, 44 © Auckland City
Inner Back Cover © Leonie Vingoe
All other photos © Stephen Picard

The sand 'Love Mandala' for New Zealand created at Piritahi Marae by Tibetan Buddhists

*Ukelele player and author
Edward 'Scotch' Paterson*

Index

The Red Herrings

*Surrealist painter
Mike Morgan*

The French crepe stall at Ostend Market

Acknowledgements

The author sincerely thanks the Auckland Public Library, the Auckland Museum and the Waiheke Historical Society for their permission to reproduce the archival black and white photographs; AA Tourism and the Auckland City Council for their maps of Waiheke; and *Gulf News* for allowing me access to their back issues.

Many thanks to Allan Mount, Simon Johnston, Aaron Putt, Liz Walters, Greg Treadwell, Peta Stavelli, Paul Monin, Nevin White, Zen Player, Steve Tetley and Leonie Vingoe for their great assistance.

Bibliography

Gulf News. Pendragon Press, 1973-2005.
Islands of the Gulf. Shirley Maddock. Collins Press, 1966.
Marine Reserves. Royal Forest and Bird Protection Society and the Underwater Club, 1991.
On Waiheke Island: a guide book. Vivienne & Stephen Picard. RSVP Publishing Company Ltd., 1993.
Passion for Earth: Earth Houses in New Zealand. Marion Bridge. Graeme North, Jackie O'Brien. David Ling Publishing Ltd., 2000.
Sites of Ecological Significance: Waiheke Island. T.D. Fitzgibbon. 1988.
Site Recording in the eastern half of Waiheke Island. E. Atwell. Gael, 1975.
Sowers of Seeds. Reverend Colin Banfield. Anglican publication, 1978.
Stony Batter: Waiheke Island ministerial inspection. Department of Lands and Survey, 1982.
The Botany of Auckland. Lucy Cranwell. Auckland Institute & War Memorial Museum, 1981.
Waiheke County. Department of Lands coastal reserves investigation, 1978.
Waiheke Island: a history. Paul Monin. Dunmore Press, 1992.
Waiheke Island: a tour. Waiheke Island Historical Society, 1983.
Waiheke Pioneers. Dixie Day. Waiheke Island Historical Society, 1983.

*Pakatoa Island from
Man O'War Bay*